# AN AMERICAN IN TEXAS
## *The Story of Sam Houston*

# AN AMERICAN IN TEXAS
## *The Story of Sam Houston*

**Peggy Caravantes**

## MORGAN
## REYNOLDS
### *Publishing, Inc.*

620 South Elm Street, Suite 223
Greensboro, North Carolina   27406
http://www.morganreynolds.com

# Notable Americans

Sam Houston

Marcus Garvey

Jimmy Carter

Ronald Reagan

Dolley Madison

Thomas Jefferson

John Adams

Andrew Jackson

Alexander Hamilton

George W. Bush

Lyndon Baines Johnson

Dwight D. Eisenhower

Ishi

Richard Nixon

Madeleine Albright

Lou Henry Hoover

Thurgood Marshall

Petticoat Spies

William Tecumseh Sherman

Mary Todd Lincoln

AN AMERICAN IN TEXAS:
THE STORY OF SAM HOUSTON

Copyright © 2004 by Peggy Caravantes

Library of Congress Cataloging-in-Publication Data

Caravantes, Peggy, 1935-
An American in Texas : the story of Sam Houston / Peggy Caravantes.—1st ed.
   v. cm. — (Founders of the Republic)
 Includes bibliographical references and index.
Contents: Early years — Houston's early military career — From leader
 to outcast — The pendulum swings — Call to war — Leader of Texas —
The war with Mexico — Texas and secession.
   ISBN 1-931798-19-2
   1. Houston, Sam, 1793-1863—Juvenile literature. 2.
Governors—Texas—Biography—Juvenile literature. 3.
Legislators—United States—Biography—Juvenile literature. 4. United
States. Congress. Senate—Biography—Juvenile literature. 5.
Texas—History—To 1846—Juvenile literature. [1. Houston, Sam,
1793-1863. 2. Governors. 3. Legislators. 4. Texas—History—To 1846.]
I. Title. II. Series.
   F390.H84C365 2003
   976.4'04'092—dc22

                         2003013257

Printed in the United States of America
First Edition

*To my children—Brian, Susan, and Jeff—with love*

# Contents

Sam Houston, 1857.

*(Courtesy of the Library of Congress.)*

# Chapter One

## Early Years

Torches of burning pine-knots in split stakes lit the three-mile trail from the lodge of Cherokee Chief Jolly to the shore of Webber's Falls. After the steamboat *Facility* edged its way to the river bank, a lone figure disembarked and walked into the chief's welcoming arms. The man was thirty-six-year-old Sam Houston, the adopted son of the chief. It was May 1829, in the Arkansas Territory.

Four months earlier, Sam had ridden the crest of popularity as governor of Tennessee with his beautiful young bride at his side. But that brief marriage had failed soon after, and Houston resigned as governor. Full of shock and bitterness, he returned to the place that nurtured him in his teenage years when he hated his life as a store clerk. When the Cherokees waiting on the shore recognized him, they began to chant his Indian name, "Colonneh! Colonneh!" His adoptive father embraced him and said, "My wigwam is yours—my home is yours—my people are yours—rest with us."

Over the next months, Sam totally reverted to Indian ways. He sported a goatee and a mustache and plaited his hair in a single braid that hung down his back. He wore a white doeskin shirt decorated with bright-colored beads and yellow leather leggings that reached his thighs. On his head he wore either turkey feathers or a figured silk headpiece. A blanket was draped across his shoulders. He refused to speak any English. Less than six months later, Sam became a citizen of the Cherokee Nation.

For the next three years, many people forgot about Sam Houston, whose formerly bright future now seemed hopeless. He had once been spoken of as a possible future president of the United States. Then, in 1832, Sam left the Cherokees and headed for Texas, where he would face challenges as big as the territory itself. There he made a name for himself as general, negotiator, president of the Republic of Texas, senator, and governor. The years in self-exile, followed by his development as a major figure in Texas history, were part of a cycle Houston repeated over and over: Whenever he fell, he always rose to greater heights. People either loved him or hated him, and his faults often overshadowed his good qualities. Continually involved in controversy, he followed his dreams and ignored the personal consequences of his decisions to remain true to his principles. A man of courage with an unconquerable spirit, he left an indelible mark on the history of Texas and on that of the entire United States.

At the age of sixteen, Sam Houston left home to live with the Cherokees on Hiwassie Island. *(Courtesy of the Library of Congress.)*

Samuel Houston, the fifth child and fifth son of Samuel and Elizabeth Houston, was born at Timber Ridge in Rockbridge County, Virginia, on March 2, 1793. The family lived on a plantation the elder Houston had inherited from his father, Robert Houston. The family had lived a quiet life there until the Revolutionary War began in 1776. Robert's son Samuel was one of the first young men to enlist from Virginia. He was a good soldier and soon became a member of the elite Morgan's Rifle Brigade. George Washington called on this group for his toughest assignments.

At the end of the war, Samuel came home with the rank of captain. He married a beautiful and wealthy eighteen-year-old girl, Elizabeth Paxton, but after seven years of military service, Samuel found plantation life boring. He joined the Virginia militia as a colonel and spent most of his days away from home. He happened to be at home for the birth of his namesake, two days before George Washington took the oath of office for his second term. It was the same year that Eli Whitney invented the cotton gin.

Colonel Houston's love of the military drove him back to duty soon after the birth of little Sam, but he returned for short visits when his duties permitted. Elizabeth Houston was thus forced to oversee the work on the plantation, so a slave girl named Peggy became the young child's caretaker. When Sam turned three, his brother William was born, followed by sister Mary the next year. By the time Sam was seven years old, he had eight brothers and sisters.

Sam did not begin school until after his eighth birthday. He learned to read and write and to do some arithmetic in the Liberty Hall Academy, a log building next to his house. A poor student, Sam preferred reading books from his father's library to going to school. Like other boys of that time, he attended school only in the fall and winter. During the spring and summer, Sam worked in the fields with his brothers. In a five-year period, he finished no more than six months of school.

Sam enjoyed his childhood—riding horseback, swimming in the river, and hunting in the woods. Sometimes he carried his father's second-best sword and pretended to kill British Redcoats and Indians. On Sundays he went to Timber Ridge Church, less than one hundred yards from his home and school.

As Sam reached his teen years, Colonel Houston went bankrupt due to the neglect of his plantation. In poor physical and financial shape, the fifty-year-old father of nine decided to leave Virginia. Like many others of his time, he planned to head west and start over in Tennessee. The Louisiana Purchase of 1803 had doubled the size of the United States and opened more possibilities for westward expansion.

In September 1806, Colonel Houston sold the Timber Ridge plantation. With the money from the sale, he acquired four hundred nineteen acres on Baker's Creek near the Great Smoky Mountains of Tennessee and bought a five-horse Conestoga wagon to transport the family's possessions. Before the family moved, Colonel Houston wanted to go on one more military tour of duty. He never returned from that trip, dying unexpectedly in Dennis Callighan's tavern on Old Kentucky Road. Sam's fifty-year-old mother decided to fulfill her husband's plans by moving her six sons and three daughters to Tennessee. The family endured many hardships as they headed west and crossed the Allegheny Mountains. At last, they arrived on the plot of land selected by the colonel.

The Houston property was only eight miles from the Tennessee River, the boundary between white settlements and the Cherokee Indians. When they first arrived, the family stayed with relatives until they could clear the land and build a two-story house. Sam's brothers began farming to provide for the family. In 1809, Sam attended the Maryville Academy for a while because he wanted to read books like the epic poem by Homer, *The Iliad*, in their original languages. When the principal refused to teach him Latin and Greek because he had not completed enough of his other studies, Sam quit school.

Sixteen-year-old Sam Houston also rebelled against farming because it required too much work and bored him. Despite his laziness, Sam's mother did not like to scold her tall, handsome son with wavy chestnut hair. Instead, she placed him as a clerk in the family store in Maryville. He did not like that job either, and one day he did not show up for work. This was not the first time that Sam had disappeared with no explanation.

Sam's brothers resented his refusal to help with the tremendous work required to run a farm and a store. When they discovered he had left without telling anyone, they started to search Sam's usual hiding places, but this time they could not find him. Several days passed with no sign of the teenager anywhere. His mother became more and more worried.

Untroubled by his family's concern, Sam had crossed the Tennessee River to join his friends, the Cherokee Indians. A band of three hundred Cherokees lived on a small island that flourished with all kinds of game, grapes, honey, nuts, and flowers. They lived in rectan-

Cherokee Chief John Jolly adopted Sam Houston and gave him the Indian name Colonneh, meaning Raven. *(Courtesy of the National Collection of Fine Arts, Smithsonian Institution.)*

gular log cabins with bark roofs and grew crops, such
as corn, beans, squash, pumpkin, tobacco, and sweet
potatoes. They had their own written language and in
many ways resembled the pioneers.

While he stayed with them, Sam learned the
Cherokee's language and wore their native dress. In the
evening, he sat around the campfire and joined in passing the long pipe. Sam admired the Cherokee leader,
Chief Oolooteka, or John Jolly as the white men called
him. The chief was a six-foot tall, handsome man in his
mid-forties. He saw much of himself reflected in Sam
and offered to adopt the boy. Houston liked the idea of
having another father since his own had died. The tribe
held a ceremony and gave Sam the Indian name
Colonneh, or Raven, which symbolized good luck in
Cherokee mythology. For the remainder of his life, Sam
considered the raven a symbol of his personal destiny.

One day, two white poachers came into the family
store in Maryville and claimed they had seen a boy
matching Sam's description on Hiwassie Island, home
of the Cherokees. Mrs. Houston sent two of her sons,
James and John, to bring Sam home. When they found
Sam, he was sitting under a tree reading Homer's *Iliad*.
The Greek story so fascinated Sam, he had already
memorized five hundred lines of the epic poem. He
often walked along the river banks with Cherokee girls,
reciting to them long passages from the book, which
they did not understand.

His brothers asked Sam why he had run away to the

Indians. Sam, who admired the Cherokees because they hunted and fished for their food, replied that "he preferred measuring deer tracks, to tape—that he liked the wild liberty of the red men better than the tyranny of his own brothers." Sam refused to return home with his brothers, where he would have to listen to their constant criticism. James and John left, believing he would follow them back, but he did not.

Instead, he enjoyed the friendship of his half-Indian friends, John and James Rogers. From them he learned the green corn dance, the hoop and pole game, and ball play, the forerunner of lacrosse. Sam relished the wild game played with as many as fifty people on each team. The object was to capture a small ball in a curved stick, carry it down the field, and throw it over the goal. There were no rules, and biting, gouging, and kneeing were common. Games became so rough that a player running down the field could be pushed, kicked, or even killed by the opponent. The Cherokees loved to bet on these games, and wagers climbed so high that people lost all their possessions, including their clothes.

A year after his brothers had found him, Sam went back to Maryville to ask his mother to make him some new clothes, since his old ones had worn out. While at home, his attitude about farming remained the same. At one point, his brothers sent him out with a team of horses to cultivate a cornfield. When they went to look for him, they found Sam on the ground next to the cornfield, reading a book while the horses nibbled grass.

While he was in Maryville, Sam got into trouble with the law. After getting drunk, Sam and a friend, Johnny Cusick, started beating on a drum just outside the window of a courtroom. When the sheriff tried to stop them, Sam got rough with the officer. For that incident, he received a large fine, which officials dropped at the end of one year. They could not collect from Sam because he had returned to the Cherokees, and no one wanted to ask his mother to pay the fine.

Sam spent three years with the Cherokees. He returned to Maryville from time to time to purchase, on credit, gifts for his Indian friends, such as gunpowder, shot, needles, and blankets. While Sam retreated into the peaceful life of the Cherokees during his late teen years, the war between France and England began to affect the United States. French Emperor Napoleon Bonaparte had crushed most of the European countries in well-planned battles. Only Britain remained for Napoleon to conquer. The French fleet, however, had not recovered from its destruction in 1805, and Napoleon could not attack the superior British navy. He decided instead to prevent any British goods from getting into other European ports. In this way he hoped to ruin the British economy.

As that war continued, both sides demanded the United States stop trading with the other. Needing more sailors, English ships stopped American vessels and impressed, or forced, American seamen to serve with the British. Napoleon Bonaparte seized ships to add to

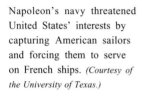

Napoleon's navy threatened United States' interests by capturing American sailors and forcing them to serve on French ships. *(Courtesy of the University of Texas.)*

his country's fleet. Congress passed laws in 1809 and 1810 to stop these practices. The United States promised to stop trading with France and Britain if they did not comply.

Napoleon agreed to the terms but continued to seize American ships. Britain held out on its agreement for another eighteen months. In November 1811, a group known as the War Hawks formed in Congress, demanding war against Great Britain. Kentuckian Henry Clay, leader of the House of Representatives, was the spokesman for this group, which hated the British. They resented Britain's impressment of American seamen. They also believed Britain had incited the Indians in the frontier wars. The War Hawks wanted the United States to fight for its independence from Britain once again. Although the Federalist Party, which represented the New England shippers, opposed such action, the majority in Congress overruled them, and the decision was made to go to war.

About this same time, when he was nineteen years old, Sam decided to move back to Maryville. Merchants refused to give him any more credit, as he needed to pay off the more than one hundred dollars in charges for the gifts he had bought the Cherokees. Sam did not want a job that involved physical labor, so he sent out announcements to the forty families living in Maryville that he would open a private school for children.

At first, the townspeople laughed at the thought of Sam Houston teaching school. Although he was an excellent speller and could recite from memory most of the twenty-four books of *The Iliad*, Sam had little formal education. However, he was confident the knowledge he had gained from reading his father's books and from his years with the Cherokees would provide him with enough experience to teach the children.

On a farm about five miles from Maryville, Sam found a broken-down, twenty-by-eighteen-foot log building in which to hold his school. Two sides of the log building had shutters that dropped down to rest on props. The dropped shutters provided both light and desks for the students. His first classes began in May

Congressman Henry Clay and the War Hawks pushed the United States Congress to declare war on the British. *(Courtesy of the Library of Congress.)*

1812, after the students had helped to plant the corn on their families' farms.

In the students' second month of school, Great Britain approached the United States about peace terms in regard to the acts of Congress in 1809 and 1810. The United States government did not inform the American public that the British had agreed to leave American ships alone. By the time the people knew about the talks, it was too late. Pushed by the War Hawks' demands, President James Madison had declared war against the British five days earlier, on June 8. The War of 1812 had begun.

In Maryville, the students continued in school until July, when they stopped to harvest the corn. Then, from August through November, students returned to school. Although at first Sam had few students, in a short time he had more than he could accept. He charged an annual fee of eight dollars, two dollars more than the average six dollars paid for a year of school. Despite the high rate, families paid the fee, divided into three parts, as instructed by Sam—one third in corn delivered to the mill, one third in cash, and one third in various colors of cotton cloth.

Sam had bright shirts made for himself from the cotton. These, plus the tight braid he wore down his back, reminded him of his Indian friends. The twenty students, ranging in age from six to sixty, all loved his stories about his life with the Cherokees. By December, Sam had paid off his debts to the Maryville merchants.

Since the cold winter weather forced the closing of the school's shutters, taking away both light and desks, Sam decided to close the school for good after having taught less than a year. Sam had earned some respect from the townspeople and had good feelings about the experience. In later years, after he had held many important state and national offices, a friend asked him which of all his positions had provided him the most pride. Sam replied that as a teacher he "experienced a higher feeling of dignity and self-satisfaction than from any office or honor which [he had] since held."

# Chapter Two

## Houston's Early Military Career

Although Sam considered becoming a real teacher, a military life appealed to him more. He knew he would need more mathematics to earn a commission as an officer, so he enrolled in the Porter Academy. When he could not understand geometry, however, he quit after only a few days' attendance. But Sam's interest in the military continued, especially as he heard more about the progress of the War of 1812. The United States had decided to meet the British on land rather than at sea, where the British reigned supreme. The United States Army had not been successful in its initial encounters with the British because the American troops were not ready for combat. America needed more soldiers.

In March 1813, some army recruiters came to Maryville to find more volunteer soldiers for the Tennessee militia. Well-dressed sergeants modeled the army uniform of white pantaloons and waistcoats, showed the crowd the rifles the recruits would use, waved banners, and played lively music. Beer and whiskey flowed with a great deal of kidding and horseplay. When the show ended, Sam took a silver dollar from the drummer's drumhead as a symbol of his intent to join the army. He wanted to fight the British. Many people, including his brothers, thought the 6-foot-2-inch Sam had disgraced the family when he enlisted as a common soldier. They believed his father's military career entitled him to an appointment as an officer.

Since Sam had not yet reached the age of twenty-one, his mother had to approve his enlistment. She gave her permission as well as a plain gold ring that had belonged to Sam's father. The good luck token had the word "Honor" engraved on the inside, and Mrs. Houston told Sam he must live by that one word. He wore the ring the rest of his life. His mother also gave him a rifle but warned him, "Remember . . . that while the door of my cottage is open to brave men, it is eternally shut against cowards." When Sam left Maryville, he bragged that the townspeople would hear about him before they saw him again.

In just a few weeks, Sam received a promotion to sergeant. When two groups of infantry combined to form a new regiment, Sam became an ensign, the lowest rank for an officer. Sam's regiment had expected to fight the British. Instead, they went to battle against some Creek Indians who supported the British army. An uprising in the South by these Indians had started the Creek Indian War. The Creeks, who lived mainly in

Alabama and Georgia, believed that white men intended to take all of their lands and destroy their Indian culture. The great Shawnee chief, Tecumseh, who fought with the British, convinced the Creeks to unite with other tribes against the settlers. The Creek leader was Red Eagle, also known as William Weatherford. On August 20, 1813, he led an attack in Alabama on Fort Mims, a temporary stockade where two rivers came together about forty miles north of Mobile. In this attack, the Creeks killed over five hundred whites. Americans retaliated by destroying an Indian village, where they killed more than five hundred warriors. Other battles followed, but the Creek War did not end until General Andrew Jackson moved his Tennessee troops toward a final showdown.

On March 27, 1814, Sam Houston was one of two thousand men that marched with Jackson toward a bend of the Tallapoosa River. Here they would face one thousand Creeks. In order to drag their two cannons with them, the army had to use axes to cut a road through the wilderness. The Creeks defended a one-hundred-acre peninsula, called To-ho-pe-ka by Indians and Horseshoe Bend by whites. Seven hundred mounted militia, five hundred Cherokees, and one hundred Creeks friendly to the Americans, surrounded the bend to prevent reinforcements or escape.

At the north end, the Indians had built a large barrier composed of three rows of heavy pine logs. Between the layers were portholes through which the Indians

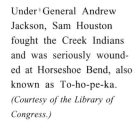

Under General Andrew Jackson, Sam Houston fought the Creek Indians and was seriously wounded at Horseshoe Bend, also known as To-ho-pe-ka. *(Courtesy of the Library of Congress.)*

could shoot. American troops fired on the defense, but their small cannons had little effect on the thick logs. At the same time, some Cherokees fighting alongside General Jackson's troops swam 120 yards across the cold, swift current of the Tallapoosa River. They found canoes the Creeks had hidden as a means of retreat. They destroyed the canoes, cutting off any chance of escape, and set fire to the wigwams near the shore in the village of To-ho-pe-ka.

As smoke rose above the island, General Jackson sent a messenger to tell the Creeks that the Americans would allow the immediate removal from the peninsula of all women and children. Then the army stormed the barrier. Through the portholes, Indians and whites fought rifle barrel to rifle barrel and knife to knife, but the Indians kept the soldiers out. Only an attack over the barricade could bring a victory. Twenty-one-year-old Sam Houston led this attack. He scaled a wall and called to others to follow him before he landed in the middle of the Creek Indians.

As he hit the ground beyond the barrier, a barbed arrow pierced his thigh. He fell to the ground but continued to fight the Creeks with his sword. The other soldiers forced the Indians to retreat to the brush, where smaller battles continued. Sam tried without success to pull out the barbed arrow. Then he asked his lieutenant, who had caught up with him, to remove the arrow. The officer tried twice and failed. Grabbing his sword and holding it above the lieutenant's head, Sam told him that if he failed on the next attempt, Sam would knock him to the earth. The officer gave a powerful tug, tearing Houston's flesh as the arrow finally came out. Blood gushed from the wound, sending Sam to a surgeon who stopped the flow of blood and bound the gash.

General Jackson had observed Sam's injury and ordered the young man not to go back into battle. Sam begged Jackson to let him continue to fight. Again Jackson ordered Sam not to return, but Sam remembered how people back in Maryville had criticized him when he joined the army. He determined either to become a hero or to die in battle. Sam rushed back into the conflict, where men fought hand to hand. The Creeks used guns, knives, bows and arrows, and tomahawks.

Savage yells and the groans of dying men filled the air. When Jackson saw so many men dying, he again sent the messenger to the Creeks with word that the Americans would spare the lives of the rest of the Indians if they would give up.

Medicine men had told the Creek Indians that the Great Spirit would help them win the battle. The Great Spirit's sign would be a cloud. Just as the messenger reached the Creeks, a cloud passed across the sun. The Indians believed this was their sign of victory, and they fired at the messenger. The battle continued. The Creeks refused to give up even when soldiers placed their swords at the Indians' chests. By the end of the day, only a few Creeks remained, hidden in a large ditch in the barricade, where the logs formed a roof. Through the portholes, they could fire at anyone who approached their position. The only way to capture them was to storm their defense. Since such an action would cost many lives, General Jackson called for volunteers.

Again Sam Houston led the charge. One rifle ball shattered his right arm. Another smashed his right shoulder. As his gun dropped to the ground, he tried to encourage others, but his fellow soldiers had taken cover instead of following him. Alone, under heavy Indian fire, Sam climbed to the top of the ravine. At about the same time, Jackson ordered the firing of flaming arrows toward the Creek defense. With the log barrier on fire, the Americans at last won the battle.

They left behind the corpses of five hundred fifty-seven Creeks. Another three to four hundred had been shot trying to cross the river or had drowned. Only forty-nine Tennessee military men died in the conflict; another 157 received wounds. This encounter ended the Creek massacres, and Sam Houston earned Andrew Jackson's lifelong admiration. In later years, Houston recalled the battle:

> The sun was going down, and it set on the ruin of the Creek nation. Where, but a few hours before, a thousand brave [warriors] . . . had scowled on death and their assailants, and there was nothing to be seen but volumes of dense smoke, rising heavily over the corpses of painted warriors, and the burning ruins of their fortifications.

After the battle subsided, a surgeon used light provided by a brush fire to remove one rifle ball from Sam's arm near his shoulder, but a second doctor refused to try to remove the other ball. He believed they should not further torture a man who would surely die before morning. All night Sam lay on a dirty blanket on the wet ground, alone and with no cover. He felt deserted because everyone ignored him, treating him as one already dead. Terrible pain gripped his body, and by the next morning Sam barely clung to life. As the troops moved out, they placed Sam on a litter and carried him sixty miles to Fort Williams. When the army moved on, they left Sam behind with some volunteer soldiers from Tennessee who cared for him in their field hospital. But these soldiers were ready to go home, so they put Sam in a rough litter between two horses that pulled him through northern Alabama and across Tennessee. Sam suffered terrible pain in his shoulder. He developed blood poisoning and ran a high fever.

Houston pleaded with the men to leave him behind so that he could die in peace, but they just gave him doses of whiskey for the pain and continued their journey. Part of the time Sam was unconscious. In May, two months after the battle, he reached his home in Tennessee. Two of the men helped him walk up the path to his mother's door. Mrs. Houston did not recognize the tall man whose skin hung on his big body, and at first she did not believe this was her son. In a cracked voice, Sam asked, "Don't you know me, Ma?" In later years, he recalled that incident, "When I reached the house of my mother, I was so worn to a skeleton that she declared she never would have known me except for my eyes."

When Sam arrived home, the Creek War had ended, but America still faced more fighting with the British. Now that Napoleon had given up his French throne, and the war in Europe was over, Britain had more soldiers to fight in America. At home, Sam slowly regained his strength. On May 20, 1814, at the age of twenty-one, he received a promotion to second lieutenant because of his bravery at the Horseshoe Bend battle. At this young age, Sam Houston had already displayed many of the qualities for which he became known in later years—

independence, leadership, courage, and a strong will.

On August 9, Andrew Jackson and chiefs of the Creek Nation signed the Treaty of Fort Jackson to bring an official end to the Creek wars. As a result of that agreement, the Creeks lost to the United States twenty-three million acres of land, about half of present-day Alabama and part of southern Georgia. That same month, the British destroyed Washington, D.C., setting fire to government buildings. In October, after a decisive American naval battle on Lake Champlain, the British agreed to talk peace. The United States and Britain reached an agreement on Christmas Eve, 1814, when they signed the Treaty of Ghent.

Sam Houston decided to stay in the military. In March, he wrote to Secretary of War James Monroe, seeking to become a regular army officer. On April 20, 1815, he received a commission as a second lieutenant in the Thirty-ninth Infantry Regiment. Sam still suffered from the wounds he received at Horseshoe Bend. An army doctor ordered him to Washington for medical treatment. There he saw the burned ruins of the Capitol and the White House. Because of his injuries, Sam had missed the January 8, 1815, British attack on New Orleans, which was fought after the official end of the war because the British forces did not yet know about the peace treaty. Sam's former commander, Andrew Jackson, defended the city so well that he lost only twenty-one American lives compared to 2,036 losses for the British. This battle made Jackson a hero, and people remembered his name and his leadership when he later ran for president of the United States.

The Washington doctors could not help Sam, so the army transferred him to the First Infantry in New Orleans on May 17, 1815. In New Orleans, Sam had surgery to remove shattered bone. He lost a great deal of blood, and because he had not yet fully recovered from his battle wounds, the operation almost killed him. Doctors sent Sam to New York for more treatment by army physicians. After he returned home, he joined the southern army in Nashville, where Andrew Jackson headed the division. Two years later, on May 1, 1817, Sam became a first lieutenant.

While Sam was recovering from his wounds, the

Andrew Jackson defeated the British at the Battle of New Orleans.
*(Courtesy of the Library of Congress.)*

Cherokees signed a treaty with the United States government, agreeing to give up 1,385,200 acres of their best land in East Tennessee. For this land, the government promised to give them five thousand dollars, with another six thousand dollars every year for the next ten years. The chiefs who signed the treaty received generous gifts, but not all of the chiefs had agreed to the treaty. Those who disagreed said the chiefs who signed had no right to speak for all of them, and some of the tribes refused to move. Others wanted to resist by force. One of the groups that opposed the treaty was that of Chief Jolly, Sam's adoptive father, who objected to moving west because of a Cherokee tradition. They believed that the Black Evil—death and misery—lived in the West, while the East was Sun Land, the true home of their gods.

Andrew Jackson learned about the years that Sam Houston had lived with the Cherokees. He believed Sam's friendship with the Cherokees, and his knowledge of their language, could aid in solving the problem. General Jackson helped to get Sam Houston appointed as a subagent with the Cherokees on October 28, 1817. Subagents represented the Indian Bureau in government affairs. The appointment presented a conflict for Sam Houston. As an officer in the United States Army, he had a loyalty to his country. He also had close ties to the Cherokees after living with them for several years and being adopted by Chief Jolly. He knew the government was determined to move the Cherokees to

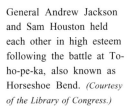
General Andrew Jackson and Sam Houston held each other in high esteem following the battle at To-ho-pe-ka, also known as Horseshoe Bend. *(Courtesy of the Library of Congress.)*

the new lands. Sam worried that if he refused the appointment and quit the military, the next subagent might treat the Cherokees badly.

Sam made his decision. He put on his Indian clothes and returned to his old life with the Indians. He convinced Chief Jolly and others that it was best for them to honor the treaty and move west. They could fight, but they would not have much of a chance against the United States army. Sam worked to make sure the government kept all of its promises to the Cherokees. He got pots, pans, blankets, needles, kettles, beaver traps, and rifles for his Indian friends before they began their long march west. The integrity Houston demonstrated in facing this complicated situation, while remaining loyal to both his country and his Cherokee friends, became the standard for Houston's future dealings as well.

Just as the bands of Cherokees started their westward journey, another problem developed. The United States had not honored a ten-year-old treaty that had moved some of the Cherokees to Arkansas. Chief Jolly's brother, Tahlontusky, led a group to Washington for a conference with Secretary of War John C. Calhoun. They wanted to get the money promised them for their land, to set the boundaries of their reservation, and to talk to the chief white man—President James Monroe. But first they had to meet with Calhoun. Jackson sent Sam Houston along as an interpreter. As an advocate for the Indians, Sam wore native dress—a cloth around

Secretary of War John Calhoun disapproved of Sam Houston's dressing as a Cherokee, and later he unjustly accused Houston of smuggling slaves across Indian land. *(Courtesy of the University of Texas.)*

his waist and a blanket over one shoulder. When the Cherokees went to meet the president, Calhoun asked Sam to stay with him. He rebuked Sam, a military officer, for dressing like an Indian. When Sam tried to explain that he had worn the Indian garb because he represented them, the angry Calhoun ordered Sam never to appear in public again unless he wore his military uniform.

A few days later, Calhoun called Sam back to his office. He stated he had received charges that Sam had helped to smuggle slaves across the Indian lands. At that time, white smugglers brought slaves from Florida, still a colony of Spain, and took them through the reservations to border settlements, where they sold them. Actually, Sam had put a stop to such smuggling, but his action angered the smugglers, who reacted by bringing the charges against him. While an investigation cleared Sam Houston's name, it revealed involvement of several congressmen in the smuggling ring. When Calhoun did not pursue these congressmen or apologize to Houston for the false charges, Sam resigned his army commission on March 1, 1818, the day before his twenty-fifth birthday. His resentment against Calhoun remained strong the rest of his life. Sam went back with the Cherokees as far as Tennessee, where he resigned as Indian subagent as well. Although he never fought the British, Sam had proved his bravery and his willingness to serve his country many times. Now, with no money and no work, Sam Houston needed a new career.

# Chapter Three

## From Leader to Outcast

In May 1818, Sam went to Nashville to study law. Although the course of study should have taken eighteen months, Sam used his extraordinary memory to finish in just six months. He passed the bar exam but had no money to set up a practice. A total stranger, Isaac Golladay, helped him to get started in Lebanon, a town about thirty miles east of Nashville. A merchant as well as the local postmaster, Mr. Golladay rented Sam a small log building at 109 E. Main Street for one dollar a month. He sold him clothes on credit, let him have postage on credit at twenty-five cents a letter, and even suggested Sam's services to the people of Lebanon. A tall, striking figure, Sam dressed well and made friends easily. Within one year, he had enough clients to pay all of his debts.

Sam made frequent trips into Nashville, where he often stopped at General Jackson's home, the Hermitage. There he met Governor Joseph McMinn, who later appointed Sam adjutant general of the Tennessee state troops with the rank of colonel. In October 1819, Sam, at the age of twenty-six, was elected prosecuting attorney for Davidson District, and he had to move to Nashville. Despite his youth, Sam made a good prosecuting attorney, but after a year, he resigned because he could make more money in the general practice of law.

On the national level, politics in Washington seethed over slavery issues. The trouble began when Missouri requested statehood. Most of Missouri was in the South, so it was expected that Missouri would be a slave state. However, because the Missouri territory extended into the North beyond the Ohio River, some Northerners wanted it to be a free state. The debate raged until Maine sought statehood as a free state. Admission of both states, one slave and one free, would maintain the balance in the Senate. The Compromise of 1820 admitted the two states with the added provision that, in all future requests for statehood, slavery would not be allowed above latitude 36° 30'. This ruling by the federal government over states' rights set the stage for the Southern states to later secede from the Union.

In Tennessee, Sam Houston's popularity continued to grow. He had gained respect as a trial lawyer, and in 1821, his fellow officers selected him as major general of the Tennessee militia. In 1822, Sam divided his time between his law practice in Nashville and the militia's headquarters in Murfreesboro. Sam worked with others in Tennessee to get the presidential nomination for Andrew Jackson. During this time, a vacancy occurred in the United States House of Representatives for a congressman from the ninth District of Tennessee. Andrew Jackson's inner circle of followers decided to back Sam Houston. Others who might have run for the position gave up when they saw Sam's support, and the thirty-year-old Houston won the seat with no opponent. Sam left for Washington, carrying with him a letter from Andrew Jackson introducing him to Thomas Jefferson.

Despite the efforts of his many friends, Jackson lost the race for the presidency in 1824. He had won the popular vote but did not have a majority of electoral votes, and the House of Representatives decided the election in favor of John Quincy Adams after Henry Clay's supporters swung their votes to Adams. Rumors spread about a deal between Adams and Clay. When

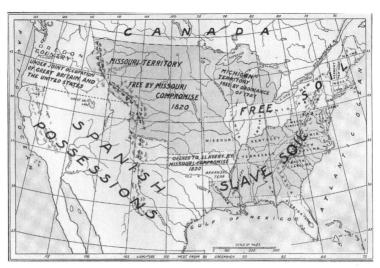

A map of the United States following the adoption of the Missouri Compromise.

John Quincy Adams defeated Andrew Jackson in the 1824 presidential election. *(Courtesy of the Library of Congress.)*

Adams appointed Clay as his secretary of state, voters saw corruption. This marked a turning point in United States elections. The people had never before been thought of as a political force. Now they would become one, and out of their actions would evolve the beginnings of the two-party political system.

Many believed John Quincy Adams's presidency was illegal as he had received only thirty percent of the popular vote. Andrew Jackson had an excellent chance of becoming president in 1828 unless he did something to offend the voting public. Sam Houston and his friends wasted no time in starting to work toward Jackson's election four years later.

In the House of Representatives, Sam supported Jackson by constantly hammering at Adams and Clay. When they gave printing contracts to newspapers that supported their administration, Houston stood in the House and thundered: "I have no objection to the principle which urges me to support my friends . . . But, then, Sir, I would be very careful who my friends were." Although the newspapers kept their contracts, Houston had raised questions about the honesty of the administration.

In 1825, Houston easily won re-election to the House for another two years, but in 1826, he decided to run for governor of Tennessee. The current governor had served three terms in a row, and under the law, could not run for a fourth. While Sam campaigned, his showy clothing added to the excitement and drama of his public appearances. He wore a ruffled shirt with a stand-up collar that covered a shiny, black patent leather tie. His costume included a black satin vest, shiny black silk pants, embroidered silk stockings, and a many-colored Indian hunting shirt. Around his waist he wore a red belt covered with beads and fastened with a silver buckle. On his feet were shoes with silver buckles, and on his head was a tall, wide-brimmed, black beaver hat.

While he campaigned for governor, Sam Houston became involved in the only duel he ever fought. For some time he had complained about the Nashville postmaster, John P. Erwin. Houston believed Erwin did not have the moral character to serve in that position. With his honor in question, Erwin hired a professional duelist, who went by the name John Smith T., to challenge Sam Houston. The duelist, who had already killed several men, presented the challenge to Houston in front of the Nashville Inn. Sam took the written dare, threw it on the ground, and then crushed it with his foot. To everyone's surprise, Smith did not attack Houston.

A Nashville lawyer, William A. White, observed the incident and believed Sam had not treated Erwin's challenge with respect. He then challenged Sam to a duel, to which Sam agreed as a matter of honor. As the challenged, Sam had the choice of weapons. He chose pistols at fifteen feet. The two men agreed to meet in a Kentucky pasture called Linkumpinch, just across the Tennessee state line, at sunrise on September 23, 1826. Although the sheriff tried to arrest the two men to prevent the duel, both men managed to escape. Sam went to the Hermitage, Andrew Jackson's home, and practiced every day for a week, although he expected to die in the duel. Jackson, who had fought several duels himself, advised Sam to keep a bullet between his teeth to give him something to bite when he fired and to steady his aim.

The two men met and Sam's first bullet struck White in the groin. Thinking he was dying, White accepted Sam's apology. After that experience, the idea of dueling so disgusted Sam that he avoided all duels in the future, even though he would receive fourteen other challenges in his lifetime.

On October 1, 1827, in the First Baptist Church of Nashville, thirty-four-year-old Sam took the oath of office to become governor of Tennessee. He had won the election by over eleven thousand votes. As governor of Tennessee, Sam continued to support Andrew Jackson's second bid for the presidency. Representing the new Democratic Party, his mentor won the election of 1828 in a landslide vote, becoming the first president from outside the Virginia and Massachusetts aristocracy. At the start of his term, Jackson brought a new spirit to government.

Americans liked Jackson because they could identify with his rise from a background of poverty. His belief that governing should come directly from the people won widespread approval. He also stressed individual liberty and equality of economic opportunity. Since Jacksonian democracy did not recognize class distinctions, everyone was invited to Jackson's victory party. Ten thousand people celebrated Jackson's inauguration with a rowdy drinking party. White House officials feared the mob would tear the rooms apart, so the staff moved the liquor outside to the lawn where the party continued.

For a while, Sam Houston's thoughts turned from politics to marriage. He had first met Eliza Allen when her uncle, a fellow member of Congress, introduced Sam to his fifteen-year-old niece. Sam visited the Allen household often, but did not fall in love with Eliza until five years later. Eliza's father, John Allen, was a wealthy Tennessee planter who encouraged the romance between his blonde, blue-eyed daughter and the handsome Tennessee governor. Although Eliza enjoyed Sam's company, she loved someone else, but the family started to pressure her because they liked the idea of having a governor in their family. Sam Houston might even become president of the United States some day. Eliza, an obedient daughter, considered her family's reasons for wanting her to marry Sam. Whether she told them about her feelings for the other man is not known. In any case, she yielded to the pressure and accepted Sam's proposal in October 1828, as they rode along the Cumberland River. Because of Sam's re-election campaign, they did not spend much time together, conducting much of their courtship through letters.

On January 22, 1829, Eliza's father escorted his twenty-year-old daughter down the magnificent staircase at their home, Allendale. For the candlelight ceremony, thirty-five-year old Sam wore a black velvet suit and a Spanish cloak lined with red satin. Except for the age difference, Sam and his bride seemed well suited to each other. The marriage so pleased Andrew Jackson that his wedding gift to the couple was the prized silver service of his recently deceased wife, Rachel.

But even from the beginning, there were problems. The couple spent their wedding night at Allendale before setting out for Nashville. Trapped by bad weather, they spent the second night with some friends, Mr. and Mrs. Robert Martin. During the night, heavy snow fell. The next morning, their hosts' two little girls got into a snowball fight with Sam. As their mother watched from a window, she remarked to Eliza that Sam seemed to be losing and suggested that Eliza go to help her new husband. Eliza may have already begun to regret her marriage and the pressure exerted by her parents because she exploded angrily to Mrs. Martin: "I wish they would kill him . . . Yes, I wish from the bottom of my heart that they would kill him."

Despite these shocking remarks from a bride of only one day, Eliza continued her journey with Sam to Nashville, where he officially announced he would run for a second term as governor. The re-election campaign occupied most of Houston's time, and he was frequently away from home. One night when he returned from a campaign event, he found Eliza burning some old love letters. A jealous Sam accused her of not being faithful to him. Eliza denied the charge. She admitted she had been cold to him because she loved someone else, but she had not been unfaithful. They argued. Then, only three months after their wedding, Eliza returned to Allendale. The angry, bewildered Sam went to his wife's family home and asked to see her. The family granted his wish with the stipulation that an older aunt be present at all times. With tears in his eyes, Sam knelt before Eliza and begged her to come home with him, but she refused. She returned his diamond engagement ring, which for years he wore in a little buckskin pouch on a leather thong around his neck.

The gossip about the breakup of the governor's marriage divided Tennessee into two camps. Neither Sam nor Eliza discussed their separation, and Houston did not deny anything said against him. He refused to allow his friends to defend him or to say anything bad about Eliza. His reply to questions was, "This is a painful, but is a private affair. I do not recognize the right of the public to interfere in it."

Neither one ever made a negative comment about the other and would not allow others to do so in their presence. They never reconciled but did not officially divorce until 1837. Eliza Houston, in later years, married Dr. Elmore Douglass, a widower much older than she. The couple had two daughters, Martha and Susie. Eliza died on March 23, 1861. Like Sam, she remained silent throughout her life about the reasons for their separation. At her request, Eliza's grave remained unmarked in the Allen burial plot in Gallatin, Tennessee, until about 1930, when a simple marker was placed there.

On April 16, 1829, the day after his unsuccessful attempt to bring Eliza back to Nashville, Sam Houston resigned as governor of Tennessee, feeling he was a ruined man. A week later he boarded the *Red Rover* and traveled to the Cherokee Nation. He later told people, "I was in an agony of despair and strongly tempted to leap overboard and end my worthless life."

Sam longed for the peace and solitude he had enjoyed when he lived with the Cherokees as a teenager. He and Chief Jolly had kept in touch but had not seen each other for eleven years. Sam needed time to heal from the double blows of losing his bride of a few months and giving up the Tennessee governorship because of his personal code of honor.

As soon as word spread that Sam had rejoined the Cherokees, a trader came to see him. He asked Sam to go see how certain government agents were cheating the Osage, Pawnee, and Choctaw tribes. After Sam spent some time with these Indians, he wrote a letter revealing the agents' double dealing to Jackson's secretary of war, John Eaton. Eaton ignored the letter. To lessen his sorrows, Houston drank heavily. As a soldier, he drank to prove his manhood. He drank to reduce the pain of the injuries he received in the battle with the Creeks. Now he drank to relieve the pain of his failed marriage.

In Washington, Houston's enemies campaigned to lower Andrew Jackson's opinion of Houston. When they told his mentor about Sam's failed marriage, his resignation as governor of Tennessee, and his return to the Cherokees, the president exclaimed, "Is the man mad?" Sam's enemies moved to seal Houston's fate. They told Jackson that all of Houston's actions were a cover-up for Sam's desire to conquer Texas, still a part of Mexico. Such rumors alarmed Jackson, who was trying to improve relations with Mexico in order for the United States to purchase Texas. He wanted to keep these negotiations quiet, however, as there was much opposition in Congress to Texas becoming a state. The entry of Texas, a slave state, would add to that group's number. Jackson worried that if Sam moved ahead with the idea of conquering Texas, people would assume Sam acted as Jackson's representative. In letters back and forth between Jackson and Houston, Sam assured Jackson he was loyal to his old friend and his only desire was to stay with the Cherokees. But Houston's enemies had succeeded in planting a seed of doubt in Jackson's mind.

As Sam continued his exile, representatives from tribes in the area sought his advice. Sam learned about their problems with treaties with the United States. Although the government owed them large sums of money for their land and had agreed to pay in gold, it gave the Cherokees pieces of paper that showed the amount of money owed them. These papers meant nothing to the Indians, and they traded them without question for blankets, gunpowder, or whiskey.

The Indians knew of Sam's friendship with Andrew Jackson and hoped he could help them in dealing with the government. But Andrew Jackson was working tirelessly to get a bill through Congress to force the removal of all Indians from eastern states to the western frontier. Jackson believed the government had made a mistake in letting the Indians operate as separate nations within the United States. There was too much risk of their joining a foreign country in war against the United States, as some had done in the War of 1812.

Sam Houston's love for his Indian brothers prevented his acceptance of their ultimate destruction by the whites. He supported Jackson in their removal because Sam believed such movement would bring the Indians the national government's permanent protection from further white encroachment. Sam decided to go to Washington as a representative of the Cherokee Nation. Dressed in native dress, Sam arrived in Washington on January 13, 1830, and received an invitation to the White House from President Jackson. Sam told Jackson about the agents who had cheated the Indians. One agent had caused the starvation and deaths of many by not giving them food. Sam's complaints resulted in the removal of five agents. This action drew much criticism because the agents had powerful Washington friends.

Houston then made a bid to distribute food and other supplies to the Indians at a cost of eighteen cents per person per day. The law said the bid must go to the lowest bidder, and the superintendent of Indian Affairs believed Sam's bid was too high. He felt food and supplies could be furnished to the Indians for seven cents per day and wanted to wait for more bids. President Jackson wanted to give Sam the bid without further delay, in keeping with the "spoils system" that prevailed during his administration. Jackson often rewarded his political supporters, but friends of the fired agents protested so strongly against Houston that Jackson eventually backed down. Houston returned to Arkansas and rejoined the Cherokee tribe.

Chief Jolly later sent Sam as his representative to a seven-day celebration called the Green Corn Dance, the most important social function in the Cherokee Nation. There Sam met the woman who would become his next wife—thirty-year-old Tiana, or Diana, Rogers, niece of Chief Jolly. Tiana, a widow, had been married to David Gentry, a respected blacksmith who had died in a battle with the Osage Indians. Only one-sixteenth Cherokee, the tall, beautiful Tiana had a gentle face, large black eyes, charm, and a quick mind. In the spring of 1830, on the Neosho River near Fort Gibson, Sam built a large, comfortable log house, which he called "Wigwam Neosho." To this house, Sam brought his new bride. The Cherokees did not care that Sam had not yet divorced Eliza. Sam and Tiana married in a civil ceremony, according to laws of the Cherokee Nation. Sam opened a trading post to support himself and his new wife, and began to prosper.

While Sam was settling back down with the Cherokees, Andrew Jackson proposed to Congress that the southeastern Indians be forced to move to public lands west of the Mississippi. Religious and political groups protested, but Congress passed the Indian Removal Act of 1830. Jackson signed the bill into law. The Cherokees at first tried to fight by challenging the act in the Supreme Court, arguing that they were an independent Cherokee Nation. The court did not recognize them as a nation and ruled against them.

During this time, Sam continued to struggle with his weakness for alcohol. In the fall of 1830, he purchased ten barrels of liquor for his post. He seemed determined to drink them all by himself. In the spring of 1831, he tried to get a position on the Cherokee Council but lost, probably because he was always drunk. At age thirty-eight, Sam Houston reached the lowest point of his career. He argued with his adoptive father about his defeat. Chief Jolly told him, "A man who is drunk is only half a man." The angry Sam struck the chief. When other Cherokees tried to hold him back, he resisted. They beat him until he staggered and dropped to the ground. He later told the council he regretted his actions and publicly asked for Jolly's forgiveness.

Sam made a trip to Nashville in 1831 to see if there was gold on some land he owned in Tennessee. On this trip he secretly visited Eliza. She told one of her former bridesmaids about the incident. A housemaid had come to the garden to get Eliza, saying a man was waiting for her in the reception room. When she entered the room, Eliza immediately recognized the disguised stranger as her husband. Sam did not know Eliza had seen through his disguise and started to talk about the weather, the river, and other unimportant matters. All the time he spoke, he stared at her face as if trying to memorize it. Eliza never indicated she knew the man was Sam. He finally left, went down to the river, got in a canoe, and paddled to the other side.

In June, Sam learned his mother was very ill, and he left for Maryville. Elizabeth had suffered multiple hardships—the deaths of two children and the mental illness of another. Her biggest disappointment, however, was the failure of her favorite son, Sam. When he arrived at her bedside, Sam knelt and cried as his mother blessed him before she died. By October, Sam had rejoined the Cherokees.

# Chapter Four

## The Pendulum Swings

In 1832, Sam Houston traveled with another group of Cherokees to Washington to present their grievances to President Jackson. Although Houston was not a delegate this time, he went with them as their adviser. He had handwritten the petition they carried. Jackson was in the midst of political turmoil over his plan to do away with the National Bank, and also faced a scandal involving a member of his cabinet. A member of the House of Representatives, William Stanberry, hoped to further disgrace Jackson by criticizing his handling of Houston's earlier bid for the Indian contract. In the House newspaper, the *National Intelligencer*, Houston read Stanberry's remarks, which hinted that Jackson had been involved in a fraud. Houston wrote to Stanberry to ask if he had been quoted correctly. Stanberry refused to give any information to a person he considered unworthy of a congressman's attention. Houston reacted by saying: "So he doesn't know me. Then I will introduce myself to the . . . rascal." Houston publicly announced his intention to beat Stanberry, who armed himself with a pistol.

Sam carried only a hickory stick he had cut at the Hermitage to make himself a cane. One dark evening, Stanberry saw Houston at a distance. Having learned that Houston was not armed, Stanberry crossed the street toward Sam. As soon as Sam saw a face in the moonlight, he asked the man if he were Stanberry. When Stanberry identified himself, Sam knocked him to the ground. He began to beat Stanberry's head and shoulders with the stick. Because of the old injury to his shoulder, Sam could not hold Stanberry and beat him at the same time. He jumped on Stanberry from behind to try to bring him to the ground. Stanberry swayed with Sam's almost two-hundred-pound weight but carried him on his back for a short distance.

When their bodies finally separated, Stanberry's hat fell off. He bent over to get it, tripped, and fell. He rolled on his back with his feet stuck up in the air. His rear end provided a new target for Sam, who continued to beat him with the stick. Stanberry pulled out his pistol and held it to Sam's chest. It misfired. Sam continued to beat the hollering Stanberry until he grew tired of it, and then he allowed Stanberry to crawl away. Stanberry suffered a broken left hand and a bruised left arm and right elbow. Later, when asked how he felt about hitting Stanberry, Houston replied, "Meaner than ever I felt in my life; I thought I had gotten hold of a great dog, but found a contemptible whining puppy."

The next morning, Houston was arrested for attacking a member of the House of Representatives. Stanberry brought four kinds of charges against Sam, hoping to disgrace him forever. Sam did not feel he had done anything wrong. Stanberry had smeared his name and had refused to answer his request for an explanation. Stanberry had carried a pistol, while Houston had only a stick. Sam hired Francis Scott Key, a Washington attorney and Jackson supporter, to defend him in the House trial. The entire House of Representatives served as a jury with the trial lasting over thirty days.

Francis Scott Key opened the trial with a weak argument, and Andrew Jackson advised Sam to take over his own defense. Jackson also told Sam to get rid of his buckskin suit and gave him money to buy clothes more suitable for appearing before the House. As the month dragged on, Sam's behavior and appearance began to win him friends. Despite the fact that he had been drunk past midnight the night before, Sam gave a brilliant speech on the last day of the trial. The House debated for four days. The trial ended with a 106-to-89 vote for the speaker of the House to publicly rebuke Sam.

The speaker, Andrew Stevenson, was an old friend of Sam's. He delivered the scolding so softly and carefully that it seemed more like an approval. Stanberry would not let the matter drop. He convinced the House to appoint a committee to determine if Houston had used fraud to try to get a contract with the Indians. Stanberry became chairman of that committee. Despite a long,

Francis Scott Key, the author of "The Star Spangled Banner," served as Sam Houston's defense attorney before the U.S. House of Representatives against the charges brought by Congressman William Stanberry. *(Courtesy of the New York Public Library Picture Collection.)*

careful search for negative information, the committee finally admitted it could find no evidence to support such a charge. Then, in a third attempt to discredit Houston, Stanberry introduced a resolution to bar Sam from the House lobby forever. As a former representative and a former governor, Houston had a right to go there. The resolution failed 90 to 101.

Stanberry turned to the courts and brought charges against Houston for beating him with the stick. The judge placed Houston on twenty thousand dollar bond. Sam could have avoided the trial if he had left Washington, but he stayed. Twenty days later, he was fined five hundred dollars and court costs. No one ever tried to make him pay, and one of Andrew Jackson's last acts as president was to cancel the fine. Before the Stanberry incident, Sam Houston had gained a reputation as a drunk. After his success in arguing before the House and receiving national attention and approval, Houston claimed new energy. He was ready for a new challenge.

Throughout Houston's stay in Washington, he and Andrew Jackson held many conversations about Sam's future. Jackson appeared willing to place Houston in an office in his administration, but Houston refused, believing such an action would bring about more accusations for his mentor. When Jackson asked Houston to go to Texas as a personal favor to try to stop Comanche raids across the American borders, Sam accepted. Houston returned to the Cherokees and announced his intention to go to Texas.

Sam had thought about going to Texas while he was still involved in the Stanberry incident. He had made some prior investments in Texas colonization when Mexico invited Americans to develop settlements. Throughout his trial, Sam exchanged letters with possible financial backers who wanted him to represent them in the purchase of land in Texas. Jackson's request that he try to bring about a peace treaty with the Comanches was the spur Houston needed to finally go. Sam invited Charles Noland, a friend, to go with him to Texas. He wrote: "I am tired of this country and sick of this life. Go with me, and I will make a fortune for both . . . I am going, and in that new country, I will make a *man* of myself again."

In late November 1832, Sam told Tiana goodbye, as she had chosen to stay with her own people rather than to go with him to live a life among strangers. He was able to sever his marriage with her more easily than with his first wife because they had been married under Cherokee tradition rather than U.S. law. She was later buried at Fort Gibson National Cemetery, with a head-stone reading "Talahina R. Wife of Gen. Sam Houston."

After his farewell, Houston mounted a small horse that had no tail. His tall body must have looked foolish on the bobtailed horse, and he complained about it as he joined two companions, Federal Marshal Elias Rec-tor and Major Arnold Harris, to head for the Red River. At the border, Major Harris finally traded horses with Houston, knowing that a tailless horse had no chance against the huge horseflies in Texas. Rector wanted to give Sam something as well, but all he had with him was a razor. When he presented the token gift, Houston said: "I except [sic] your gift, and mark my words, if I have luck this razor will someday shave the chin of a president of a republic." That statement revealed Sam's high hopes for his future in the new land. He crossed the border into Texas on December 10, 1832.

Just a few years earlier, in 1829, Andrew Jackson had told the United States minister in Mexico to make an offer to buy Texas. Jackson's enemies assumed the president was now sending Houston to conquer the territory. When Houston entered Texas, he knew little of the struggle that had been going on there since Stephen F. Austin settled an American colony of three hundred in the Mexican territory. Like Sam Houston,

Stephen Austin's father, Moses, received a land grant to colonize a portion of Texas, at that time a possession of Mexico. Upon his father's death, Stephen fulfilled Moses's dream by establishing several colonies of Americans in the new territory. *(Courtesy of the Library of Congress.)*

Austin had attained much recognition before his thirtieth birthday, but the similarities ended there. At the time of the death of his father, Moses Austin, Stephen was only twenty-seven years old. Already successful as a legislator, businessman, and judge, Stephen then took on his father's dream to settle colonists in Texas.

Stephen had a reputation for patience, understanding, determination, and honesty. These traits helped him choose an area near the Brazos and Colorado Rivers to settle the colonists. He had strong rules for the colony—no drinking, no gambling, no swearing, and no idling. Sam Houston would never have qualified to be included among the initial settlers, who began arriving in December 1821.

In 1824, Mexico passed a New Colonization Law. The state of Coahuila y Texas declared itself open to all foreign immigration. Stephen F. Austin was no longer the only person that could bring people into Texas. He did establish several other colonies over the next few years, earning himself the name "Father of Texas." Austin felt a real responsibility to his settlers. He saw his job as providing a future for families, and he became both their friend and adviser. A small, slender man with a quiet, soft-spoken voice, he believed in discussing issues rather than in arguing or fighting. He had the ability to get along with people of other cultures than his own. Both the Texas colonists and the Mexicans trusted and respected him.

Around the time Houston arrived in Texas, the Mexican government was in turmoil due to power struggles between Mexican Presidents Anastasio Bustamante and Antonio Lopez de Santa Anna. Bustamante had been president from 1830 to 1832, before Santa Anna led a revolt against him and became president in 1833. By 1837, Bustamante was back in power once again.

It was Santa Anna who would pose the greatest threat to Texans over the course of his career, and he would become Houston's greatest military rival. Charismatic and bold, Santa Anna became known as "the Napoleon of the West." Short and pot bellied, prone to bouts of melancholy, he might have seemed an unlikely candidate for military hero, but he was a born leader, capable of mounting brilliant and ruthless assaults. He could also be reckless, however, and his ability to govern never matched his skill at leading troops in battle. Houston later praised Santa Anna as a genius, and gave much credit to luck for his own successes against the Mexican leader.

Austin got caught not only in the upheavals caused by rival Mexican leaders, but also in the conflict between the settlers and the Mexican government. Texans wanted a political system like the one they had left behind in the United States. They wanted trial by jury, and the right to be free on bail while awaiting trial. Under Mexican law, local military officials could deny both of these rights. Two other issues brought Texans into conflict with the Mexican government—slavery and religion. Texans worried that Mexico would end slavery, and they resented having to become Roman Catholics in order to buy land.

A series of small battles erupted between Texans and Mexicans over taxes on imported goods and over the Mexicans' use of the Texans' slaves to work at the Mexican fort. William Barrett Travis, a twenty-six-year-

Mexican President Antonio Lopez de Santa Anna, known as "the Napoleon of the West," led the Mexican army against the Americans in Texas. *(Courtesy of the Library of Congress.)*

old lawyer from South Carolina, and Patrick C. Jack from Alabama, led the settlers' complaints. When the fort commander arrested them, the settlers marched on the fort and forced the freeing of the two men. Texans began to arm themselves. The Mexicans reacted by trying to prevent a ship from delivering its cargo, a cannon, to the Texans. On June 26, 1832, the Mexicans and Texans had their first battle at Velasco. After ten hours, the Mexicans surrendered, and Mexican soldiers began to leave Texas. Soon the only Mexican soldiers remaining were at San Antonio and Goliad.

News reached the Texans that Santa Anna had overthrown Mexican President Bustamante and established himself as dictator. Stephen F. Austin and other Texas leaders convinced a Santa Anna representative that Texas was loyal to the new dictator. They believed the time had come to ask for the government reforms they desired. Texans decided they wanted to separate from Coahuila and become a state by themselves.

By this time, Sam Houston had arrived in Nacogdoches, Texas, and had observed the settlers. In a letter to Andrew Jackson, Sam wrote that the majority of the people in Texas would like to be a part of the United States. With Mexico always in revolution, they had no laws and no government to protect them. Houston believed that if the United States did not make a move, England would obtain Texas. He stated that in his five hundred or more miles of travel across Texas, he had found it "the finest country . . . upon the globe." He concluded his letter by telling Jackson: "It is probable that I may make Texas my abiding place! In adopting this course, I *will never forget* the Country of my birth." Jackson did not respond to the letter.

In April 1833, Texans elected delegates to a convention at San Felipe to declare their statehood. The Nacogdoches settlement elected Sam Houston as its representative to the San Felipe Convention. Houston chaired the committee charged with writing a constitution, while another committee composed a list of reasons for separation from Coahuila. Although the delegates chose three men to present their petition to the Mexican congress, Stephen F. Austin was the only one who traveled to Mexico. He found the government once again in chaos and dictator Santa Anna in hiding. Austin could not get a hearing on the petition. After nearly six months of fruitless attempts, Austin wrote to the council in San Antonio on October 2, 1833, urging Texans not to wait any longer for Mexico's approval. All districts should join together and organize a state according to the Constitution of 1824, which had favored democracy and local self-government. Then, as Austin started for home, he was arrested and thrown into prison. His letter never arrived in San Antonio.

While Austin was in Mexico, Sam Houston bought property in Nacogdoches and started working as an attorney, representing eastern United States land investors. He joined the Catholic Church in order to own property and to practice law. He also found a new girlfriend, Anna Raguet, the seventeen-year-old daughter of Henry Raguet, a storekeeper. The beautiful, well-educated young woman was fluent in several languages. Sam asked her to teach him Spanish because he believed that a successful Texas lawyer should speak that language. He did not make much progress with the lessons or with Anna, who had another boyfriend as well. For several years the other young man, Robert Anderson Irion, a local doctor, kept up a friendly competition with Sam for Anna's attention. In November 1833, Sam had another lawyer, Jonas Harrison, ask local authorities to grant him a divorce from Eliza because of the length of their separation and of the lack of hope for solving their problems. Because he was now Don Samuel Pablo Houston, a Catholic, his request fell under the rule of the church, in whose eyes Sam remained officially married until 1837.

At this time, Houston was living quietly in Nacogdoches. He knew neither about the new turmoil in Mexico nor about the trouble facing his Cherokee friends back in the United States. By 1835, the Cherokees were still divided about white takeover of their lands. Chief John Ross and the majority of about sixteen thousand Cherokees in northern Georgia fought against giving up their lands, but a small minority of about five hundred, led by Major Ridge, supported the westward move and signed the Treaty of New Echota in December 1835. This gave Andrew Jackson the legal document he needed to move the Indians beyond the Mississippi to Oklahoma. Although such orators as Henry Clay and Daniel Webster argued against the treaty, the Senate passed it by one vote. The move would begin.

# Chapter Five

## Call to War

In Texas, people also divided into two camps. One group wanted independence, and the other wanted to keep peace with Mexico at all costs. Then word came that Santa Anna had reduced the military to one soldier for every five hundred Texans. All other men had to give up their guns. This ruling caused great anxiety because guns served as protection as well as a means of getting food. Houston at first advised the people to calm down and wait before acting. He changed his mind after the Mexicans released Stephen F. Austin. When Austin arrived back in Texas, he said: "War is our only resource. There is no other remedy. We must defend our rights, ourselves, and our country by force of arms."

On September 14, 1835, Sam Houston served as chairman of a gathering in Nacogdoches to discuss calling representatives from all over the state to a meeting. On October 2, fighting began at Gonzales when Mexican troops from San Antonio tried to take a six-pound brass cannon away from the town. The cannon, which the one hundred and sixty settlers used for protection against Indians, symbolized their ability to defend themselves. Over their thatched roofs, they stretched a banner that read, "Come and Take It." When the one hundred Mexicans did try to take it, Gonzales citizens fired on them. War had begun. News of the rebellion reached Nacogdoches, where the local committee named Sam Houston commander-in-chief of the East Texas army.

At the same time, the colonists' leaders met at San Felipe to form a temporary government by electing a council of representatives. This attempt to form a new government was the final challenge to Santa Anna. He sent his brother-in-law, General Martin Perfecto Cos, to Texas to put down the Texan rebellion. Stephen F. Austin, who was elected commander-in-chief of the Texas force, led his forces to Gonzales and sent out a call for volunteers to join him there.

Sam Houston heard about Austin's call and used his last five dollars to get a rider to spread the word about Austin's need for volunteers to capture the Alamo, the last Mexican stronghold in Texas. On October 13, 1835, Austin started toward San Antonio with 350 soldiers to attack the Mexicans before Texan reinforcements arrived. Sam Houston considered Austin's move unwise and did not at first join the advance. This hesitation caused many to call Houston a coward. When Austin and his men reached the San Antonio River, eight miles from the town, they stopped to wait for reinforcements. Austin sent a flag to General Cos and demanded surrender. The experienced general had fourteen hundred soldiers with him at the Alamo, a former Spanish mission used by the Mexicans as a fortress. Cos refused to accept the flag and started to set up barricades.

When Sam Houston arrived with his troops from East Texas, Austin asked Houston to take over as commander-in-chief. Houston refused, saying the troops would not like someone else replacing the person the men had selected to lead them. Houston tried to discourage Stephen F. Austin from attacking San Antonio, but Austin ignored the advice. Austin now had about one thousand men in his command, and he moved them north of San Antonio to blockade the town. While Austin waited to attack until he received some heavier guns, soldiers came and went at will since there was no set enlistment period. Sam Houston left with some other delegates to go back to San Felipe to organize the new state government.

Postponing the attack on San Antonio disappointed many of the soldiers. Forty-seven-year old Colonel Ben Milam, a Kentucky native, rallied the disappointed soldiers, asking, "Who will go with old Ben Milam to San Antonio?" Three hundred volunteers joined him for five days of fierce fighting against General Cos and the Mexican troops. On December 10, 1835, General Cos surrendered, and he and his remaining soldiers were allowed to return to Mexico with two cannons and enough weapons to protect them from Indians. Only twelve Texans died, while another eighteen were wounded. Among the dead was Ben Milam, who was killed in the first day of the battle. With great optimism, many of the volunteer soldiers returned to their homes, leaving only a few hundred at the Alamo. They believed, that with all of the Mexican soldiers gone from Texas, the war was over.

Fifty-five delegates, representing thirteen towns, met at San Felipe on November 3, 1835, to organize their new government, the Permanent Council. The convention appointed Sam Houston, dressed in his usual buckskin pants and wearing a Mexican serape, to form a committee with eleven others and write the constitution. On November 7, the Texans declared themselves a separate state; on November 13, they adopted the state constitution. In a 54-to-1 vote, the provisional government elected Sam Houston major general of the army. Houston tried to organize an army, but arguments among the council members about the nature of the war with Mexico prevented him from putting out a call for volunteers until December.

Part of the council favored fighting for their rights as Mexican citizens while others wanted to fight for independence from Mexico. Because he feared an attack by Santa Anna, Houston hoped to recruit five thousand men by offering bonuses of land and money. As the San Felipe government erupted into chaos, he had a hard time holding his recruits, some of whom wanted to go back to the United States. The council ordered Sam Houston to move his headquarters to Washington-on-the Brazos, a small settlement forty miles north of San Felipe. Houston knew the council was moving him out of the way but obeyed the orders. Then the council approved an expedition to Matamoras, where many believed they could gain land providing a path into Mexico's interior. Houston believed the expedition was merely an excuse to loot the town. The council ignored Houston and named Colonels James Fannin and Francis Johnson as independent military agents responsible to no other officer.

Having had no luck with the council in stopping the Matamoras expedition, Houston went to Goliad, where he addressed the soldiers. He begged them to withdraw from the attack. As he spoke, a messenger came with news that two of Santa Anna's generals had crossed the Rio Grande into Texas. James Bowie, soldier and Kentucky frontiersman, arrived to recruit volunteers to defend the Alamo. Only about thirty men went with him.

On January 17, 1836, Houston wrote to Governor Henry Smith. He requested Smith's consent to blow up the Alamo and abandon San Antonio de Bexar:

> I have ordered the fortifications in the town of Bexar to be demolished, and, if you should think well of it, I will remove all the cannon and other munitions of war . . . blow up the Alamo, and abandon the place, as it will be impossible to keep up the station with volunteers.

Houston did not believe men should be shut up in forts where they could not receive reinforcements or supplies. Smith did not give his approval.

Houston himself did not go to the Alamo because he still hoped to prevent the attack on Matamoras. Instead he went to Refugio, where he met Francis Johnson and James Fannin. The two men said they had orders from the council to replace Sam Houston as leader of the armies and to lead an attack on Matamoras. Houston refused to go with them to Matamoras, not wanting his name connected to a project he did not believe in. He talked to the volunteers and told them they did not have to go either. He convinced about two hundred of them, leaving only sixty or seventy to go with Johnson and Fannin.

In February, having been relieved of his command, Houston went back to Nacogdoches to seek election as a delegate to the Washington-on-the-Brazos convention, scheduled to begin on March 1, 1836. While in Nacogdoches, Houston visited the Raguet family. Twenty-year-old Anna promised to make Sam a silk sash for his uniform. This time Nacogdoches voters did not select Sam as a delegate, but the residents of Refugio, a place he had visited only one time, chose him to represent them. He spent the rest of February with the Cherokees in Northeast Texas, and signed a treaty guaranteeing the Indians could keep their lands as long as they did not take sides in the fight between the Texans and Mexicans. He returned to Nacogdoches, collected

Jim Bowie, along with William Travis, led the Americans who died defending the Alamo. *(Courtesy of the Daughters of the Republic of Texas Library.)*

his silk sash from Anna, and started for Washington-on-the-Brazos to help organize the new government.

On February 28, the day before Houston arrived at Washington-on-the-Brazos, a messenger delivered William B. Travis's letter stating the Alamo was besieged by Santa Anna and more than one thousand Mexican soldiers. In his letter, Travis pleaded for immediate help as the enemy was receiving daily reinforcements. Travis had assumed command of the regular army at the Alamo after the former commander, Colonel James Clinton Neill, left to go home to Bastrop, Texas, due to illness in his family. At his departure, arguments erupted over whether Travis or James Bowie should assume Neill's command. To prevent further disruption, Travis and

Bowie agreed to share the leadership role. Travis would command the regular army and Bowie the volunteers.

As delegates to the convention arrived in Washington-on-the-Brazos, they heard about Santa Anna's advance into Texas. This news caused some of them to question Houston's removal as commander-in-chief. Many had confidence in Sam's ability to lead. On March 2, 1836, Houston's forty-third birthday, the Texans signed their Declaration of Independence and became the Republic of Texas. Two days later, the delegates elected Sam commander-in-chief of the armies of the Republic.

Houston vowed to gather troops to go to Travis's aid. Only Sam knew that if the governor had approved the request to blow up the Alamo and retreat, the men would not be trapped there now. Houston decided to go to Gonzales, where a few troops remained, and move toward the Alamo. Unsure of how large an army remained in Gonzales, Houston started to gather more recruits. Because Houston had convinced so many of the soldiers to drop out of the expedition, Fannin had not gone to Matamoras after all. Houston sent a young messenger, Cameron, to Colonel Fannin at Goliad with instructions for Fannin to meet Houston at Gonzales.

On his way to Gonzales, seventy-six miles from the Alamo, Houston stopped, got off his horse, and put his ear to the ground in the manner he had learned from the Cherokees. Travis had written that as long as the Alamo could hold out, he would fire signal guns every morning at sunrise. For several days these sounds had trav-

At the battle of the Alamo, all 188 defenders were killed by Santa Anna's forces.
*(Courtesy of the Daughters of the Republic of Texas Library.)*

eled two hundred miles across the prairie. Now Houston listened in vain and feared bad news from the Alamo because he could no longer feel the vibrations in the ground. The morning firing had stopped.

Houston arrived in Gonzales to discover his army consisted of 374 men, only fifty of them with horses. Then word came that the Alamo had fallen after a thirteen-day siege, and that all 188 defenders had been killed. Later reports revealed that as many as seven defenders had lived through the battle, only to be executed at Santa Anna's orders. The only survivors were some women, children and black servants who had not fought. To avoid panic among his soldiers, Sam Houston pretended not to believe the report and arrested the messengers as Mexican spies. Most of the men had joined the army to fight at the Alamo, not to serve under Houston. Twenty of the soldiers left to take care of their families, who had lost loved ones at the Alamo.

Houston sent new orders to Fannin, who had not yet left Goliad, to blow up that fort, dump the artillery in the river, and retreat to Victoria. He further instructed him to send one-third of his men to Houston at Gonzales. Sam Houston's plan was to retreat to East Texas rather than face Santa Anna at the scene of his recent victory. Houston also hoped the enemy would divide its forces as they chased the Texans.

On March 13, 1836, a forty-nine-year-old scout named Erastus "Deaf" Smith rode into Houston's camp with three survivors of the Alamo—Susannah Dickinson, her fifteen-month-old baby girl Angelina, and William Travis's black servant Joe. The blood of her husband and other Alamo defenders covered Mrs. Dickinson's clothes. She said Santa Anna had sent her to let Sam Houston know what had happened to the Alamo defenders and to tell him that everyone who fought Mexican authority would face the same fate. If the Texans wanted to be spared, they had to lay down their arms at once. Another scout reported that Santa Anna was moving toward Gonzales.

Houston had trouble holding together a scared army in retreat. He received word that Fannin had ignored his orders and refused to leave Goliad. Houston remained resolute not to go toward San Antonio but to retreat about fifty miles east to Burnham's Crossing on the Colorado River, where they would face their enemy. He wrote to James Collingsworth, chairman of the military committee of the new republic: "If only three hundred men remain . . . I will die with them or conquer." But President David G. Burnet and his cabinet panicked and moved to Harrisburg on Buffalo Bayou, an action that did little to build the confidence of the retreating soldiers. President Burnet sent this message to Houston: "The enemy are laughing you to scorn. You must fight them. You must retreat no farther. The country expects you to fight. The salvation of the country depends on you doing so."

Then came word that Fannin had surrendered after a bloody battle. The soldiers wanted to stop retreating and attack. Houston not only did not stop but ordered a further retreat, bringing about talk among the soldiers of overthrowing his command. Some refused to march any further. For three days, Houston pushed the men through heavy rain, covering about eighteen miles. Only nine hundred remained of the thirteen hundred men who had started with him five days earlier. During this retreat, the soldiers heard that on Palm Sunday, March 27, Santa Anna executed Fannin and three hundred and ninety of his men after they had surrendered. Santa Anna was carrying out his threat to destroy Texas.

Houston's retreat, the government's flight to Harrisburg, and news of Fannin's defeat and execution caused a panic among the settlers, who fled in every direction.

This wild stampede to avoid Santa Anna's armies became known as "The Runaway Scrape." Only Sam Houston and his soldiers provided any hope for the Republic. The strength of the army changed daily, with volunteers coming and going due to desertions and men going home to care for their families. On March 28, Houston camped about one mile from San Felipe. The next day, he moved twenty miles west to the plantation of Jared Groce, a rich man who could give the army some supplies. The steamer *Yellow Stone* was also anchored there and could carry the men across the swollen Brazos River. Sam Houston told no one his plans. Though if he had done so, he might have relieved some of the soldiers' fears.

As rain delayed Santa Anna's advance, Houston used these days of retreat to organize and train his soldiers. He created a medical unit and a scouting unit led by "Deaf" Smith. On April 7, 1836, Santa Anna reached San Felipe and for four days tried to cross the Brazos River. He finally gave up crossing there on the same day that Houston received two six-pound cannons from the citizens of Cincinnati, Ohio. During the next two days, Houston moved his army across the Brazos, using the *Yellow Stone* and a small sailboat. Then he faced a fork in the road. One branch led to Nacogdoches and the Sabine River, where they could cross into the United States. The other led to Harrisburg, where Santa Anna had arrived after crossing the river at Fort Bend. Tension mounted among the soldiers as everyone waited for his decision. They were tired of retreating and wanted to fight. Some officers threatened to overthrow Houston if he picked the Sabine route. He chose the Harrisburg route, but several hundred soldiers did not want to go there, so Houston was left with even fewer soldiers to face Santa Anna. Now the Texans began to chase the Mexican army instead of retreating from them.

Sam Houston's troops covered fifty-five miles in two-and-a-half days and reached Buffalo Bayou, opposite Harrisburg, which they found in ashes. Santa Anna had already passed that way. As the army rested, "Deaf" Smith captured a Mexican scout, who told them Santa Anna had headed toward Galveston Island. Houston knew that Santa Anna had to cross Vince's Bridge on Buffalo Bayou at Lynch's Ferry to get to the island. That night, Houston studied maps of the area, and the next morning gave an inspiring speech to his troops, telling them victory was certain. "Remember the Alamo!" became their battle cry.

The Texans crossed Buffalo Bayou and found the cold ashes of Santa Anna's campfires near the place where the bayou flowed into the San Jacinto River. Houston positioned his troops in a wood of oak trees near Lynch's Ferry and placed his cannons, the Twin Sisters, loaded with broken horseshoes, on the edge of the trees. The woods formed the boundary of a swamp and a prairie that Santa Anna would have to cross to reach the ferry to Galveston Island.

The two armies were ready to meet. The Texans fired

one cannon and then the other. The Mexican cannon, called Golden Standard, answered, but was damaged by the Texan volley. Santa Anna decided not to fight the Texans directly and sent soldiers to bring back their crippled cannon. For the first time in thirty-eight days, Sam Houston slept all night on the ground without a blanket and with his saddle for a pillow. His soldiers were nervous and could not understand why he held back from attacking the nearby enemy. But Sam Houston was familiar with the Mexicans' habit of taking siestas in the afternoon. Figuring the Mexican troops must be as exhausted as his own men, Houston waited. He wrote a letter to Henry Raguet: "This morning we are in preparation to meet Santa Anna. It is the only chance of saving Texas. We will have only about seven hundred to march with, besides the camp guard. We go to conquer. It is wisdom growing out of necessity to meet the enemy now; every consideration enforces it. No previous occasion would justify it."

Then he sent scouts "Deaf" Smith, Jack Coker, and John Garner to destroy Vince's Bridge, cutting off all means of retreat for both armies. At 3:30 in the afternoon on April 21, 1836, Houston formed a line of infantry one-man deep, spread across a thousand yards. The soldiers carried rifles, tomahawks, and Bowie knives. Texans in the center of the line carried the white silk flag of the Republic, with its five-point azure star and the motto *Uni Libertas Habitat Ibi Nostra Patria*, meaning "Where liberty lives, there is our homeland."

This painting, *The Surrender of Santa Anna* by William H. Huddle, hangs in the State Capitol of Texas.

Houston gave the order to advance but made his soldiers hold their fire until they got within sixty yards of the Mexican line of defense. The soldiers did not know that Santa Anna and his troops were asleep after an all-night forced march and that before going to sleep, the Mexicans had stacked their guns instead of keeping them nearby because the Mexican general had not believed the Texans would attack.

Caught by surprise, the Mexicans tried to respond to the sudden shouts and bugle calls. About forty yards from the Mexican line, Houston's huge white stallion, Saracen, went down. Houston landed on his feet and grabbed a riderless horse. Then a three-ounce copper ball hit him just above his right ankle. The second horse was shot from under him with at least five musket balls in its chest. Houston mounted his third horse of the day. The battle itself lasted less than twenty minutes with only two Texans killed and another twenty-four wounded, six of whom later died. In the surprise onslaught, 630 Mexicans died, 208 were wounded, and 730 were taken prisoner.

As the sun went down, Sam Houston fainted from the serious injury to his right leg. Surgeons cut away his blood-filled boot and worked to repair the wound from which they removed twenty pieces of bone. As they worked, Sam created a garland of magnolia leaves and wrote on a card: "To Miss Anna Raguet, Nacogdoches, Texas: These are laurels I send you from the battlefield of San Jacinto. Thine. HOUSTON."

All day, soldiers brought in prisoners who had tried to escape. But the prize captive—Santa Anna—was not among them. That evening, a patrol of five soldiers rode into camp. Mounted on a horse behind twenty-year-old Joel W. Robinson was a wet, dirty man wearing ordinary clothes—a skin cap, a round jacket, pants of coarse blue cotton, and common shoes. The patrol had found him sitting on a tree stump near the destroyed bridge at Vince's Bayou. He seemed harmless, so the patrol started to put him with the other prisoners. But the captured Mexican soldiers began to raise their hats and shout: "El Presidente! El Presidente!" The prisoner

then asked to see Sam Houston, to whom he surrendered as Sam lay in great pain on a blanket under a tree.
Houston's soldiers wanted to kill Santa Anna right there,
but Houston stopped them. He realized that Santa Anna
was their bargaining tool with Mexico to declare Texas
an independent republic. Houston told Santa Anna that
his life would be spared if he sent his troops home and
surrendered all Mexican claims to Texas. Santa Anna
agreed.

# Chapter Six

## Leader of Texas

Although he had won a decisive battle, Sam Houston still endured criticism for the way he had retreated. The wound he sustained during battle became painfully infected, and in order to save his life, Houston went to New Orleans, where army doctors could provide better treatment. While he was out of Texas, he assigned temporary command of the army to Secretary of War Thomas Jefferson Rusk. Just before Houston left for New Orleans, Santa Anna signed an armistice and agreed to negotiate a permanent treaty to recognize Texas's independence. But the unorganized Texas government could not follow through, and the incapable David G. Burnet, president of the interim government, tried to appoint Mirabeau B. Lamar to command the army in place of Rusk. In a mass meeting, soldiers rejected Lamar by a vote of 1,500 to 179. Then Santa Anna tried to commit suicide with an overdose of morphine, believing he was going to be killed. He was foiled in his attempt by Dr.

James A. E. Phelps, on whose plantation Santa Anna was being held prisoner. President Andrew Jackson wanted to interview Santa Anna, so he was sent to Washington. After the two men talked, Jackson allowed Santa Anna to return to Mexico on the condition that the Mexican leader would retire.

On July 2, 1836, Rusk wrote to Houston and begged him to return to Texas, despite the condition of his leg, so that he could bring the army under control. Many of the newest soldiers had come to Texas to fight in a war. When they arrived and found the war had ended, large numbers started a movement to make their own war by invading Mexico. By mid-August, Sam Houston had returned from Louisiana and had the army under control. Houston became so popular with the soldiers that they took up a collection and bought Santa Anna's fancy saddle for him. In addition to calming the army, Houston soothed Indian tribes ready to go to war with Texas because of lies told to them by the Mexicans. The Texas government was close to collapse, with widespread rumors about an attempt to overthrow Burnet. The panicked president called for a general election on September 5, 1836.

Houston supported Thomas Rusk for president, but his thirty-three-year-old friend chose not to run. He believed he was too young to hold such an important position. The first to announce their candidacy for president of the Republic were Henry Smith, a former governor in the provisional government, and Stephen F. Aus-

Mirabeau B. Lamar served as vice president under Sam Houston, and then served as the second president of the Republic of Texas. *(Courtesy of the Rosenberg Library.)*

tin. As the campaign progressed, neither man appeared strong enough to unite Texas, and Sam Houston started to receive letters encouraging him to enter the race. Eleven days before the election, Houston announced he was a candidate for president. Smith and Austin continued to campaign rigorously. Though Houston campaigned very little, when the voting ended, Austin had received 587 votes; Smith, 743; and Sam Houston, 5,119. To Houston's disappointment, Mirabeau B. Lamar was elected vice president. In the same election, ninety-two percent of Texans favored their annexation to the United States, by a vote of 3,277 to 91.

Although the constitution named the second Monday of December 1836 as the date for the new president to take office, Burnet unexpectedly resigned on October 22 at Columbia, Texas, where the government had moved in September. At 4 P.M. that same day, Sam Houston, seated at a simple table covered with an old blanket, took the oath of office as the first elected president of the Republic of Texas. He could at last use Elias Rector's razor when he shaved the next morning.

As the new Texas president, Sam Houston faced many problems: no money, land issues with the Cherokees, and an army filled with rebels who had not been paid in months. Texas needed either annexation by the United States or recognition as an independent state from Great Britain and France. These countries' acceptance of Texas's independence was necessary for trade and for receiving money and loans. In the United States, many people opposed the annexation of Texas because they did not want to bring another slave state into the Union. Others opposed it because they felt that such a step would lead to a war with Mexico, which did not recognize Texas's independence. Houston counted on support for annexation from his old friend Andrew Jackson, who would soon be leaving office as president of the United States.

This did not occur, however, because to recognize Texas would have set off the explosive slavery issue at a time when Jackson was campaigning for his handpicked successor, Martin Van Buren. On March 3, 1837, his last day in office, Jackson finally recognized the Republic of Texas, but in the transition between the end of

As president of the Republic of Texas, Sam Houston lived in the Executive Mansion in Houston. *(Courtesy of the University of Texas Library.)*

Jackson's term and the start of Van Buren's term, the United States suffered a financial collapse, the Panic of 1837. Part of the collapse had to do with Jackson's economic policies, including the destruction of the National Bank. The Panic, combined with the bitter controversy over slavery, caused Congress to turn down Texas's bid to join the Union. Houston declared that Texans would not beg, and he dropped the issue for the next four years.

Meanwhile, even more settlers headed to Texas. While the Republic had once welcomed immigrants, newcomers were now viewed as one more financial burden on the new government, which already had a debt of $1.25 million. Houston had to deal with securing a lasting peace with the Comanches and Caddoes, and resolving land issues with the Cherokees, as new settlers to Texas moved on to land the Indians believed was theirs. In exchange for peace with the Indians, Sam Houston promised their land would not be taken away, and he created "ranging groups" that roamed the state to be sure promises were kept on both sides. These men became the forerunners of the Texas Rangers. Houston solved the problem of having no money to pay the army by sending all but six hundred of them on vacation for an indefinite period of time. Had he dissolved the army, he would have needed money for separation pay.

On a more personal level, Sam Houston had never liked the primitive government facilities at Columbia. The area for the president was a one-room office with a small fireplace. If Houston had an overnight visitor, the guest slept on the one cot while Houston slept on the floor. The meeting accommodations for senators and representatives were just as primitive. Then two brothers, John K. and Augustine C. Allen, offered to rent the government a two-room log cabin near Harrisburg. They called their settlement Houston, and in November 1837, it became the new capital of Texas.

The settlement, which grew rapidly as more and more people moved there, was a hard-drinking town. This suited the hard-drinking Sam Houston, who frequently drank until he was unconscious. He never admitted he had a drinking problem, though, and during the first week of January 1838, Houston made a bet with Augustine Allen that he could stay sober until the end of that year. He tried, but faced too many temptations to drink at all of the capital city's events. By spring, he had lost the bet and owed Allen a five-hundred-dollar suit of clothes.

While Sam Houston was prospering in Texas, his old friend Andrew Jackson was mistreating Houston's other friends, the Cherokees. After the signing of the Treaty of New Echota, the government began the removal of about fifteen thousand Georgia Cherokees to Oklahoma. General Winfield Scott arrived at New Echota on May 17, 1838, with seven thousand men. With rifles and bayonets, they forced all of the Cherokees—men, women, and children—from their homes and herded them into temporary, poorly constructed forts. The Cherokees lacked sufficient food as they marched the thousand miles to Oklahoma, and many died along the way.

Cherokee Chief John Ross finally persuaded General Scott to let him lead his own people. When Scott agreed, Ross divided the Cherokees into smaller groups. He had the groups move separately through the wilderness so that they could hunt for food. His actions helped reduce the loss of life, but even so, about four thousand Cherokees died as a result of the long, hard trip. The removal journey and its route came to be known as "The Trail of Tears." Chief Ross must have thought many times about Andrew Jackson's promise to him several years earlier in Washington. At that time, Jackson told him, "You shall remain in your ancient land as long as grass grows and water runs." One can only wonder how Sam Houston, adopted son of the Cherokees, remained so loyal to Andrew Jackson. At one time, Houston agreed with the westward movement of the Indians because he believed it would afford the Cherokees the permanent protection of the United States government. But surely a man of his intelligence did not believe that these ongoing, forced moves benefited his Indian brothers.

Before long, Sam Houston's term as president of the Republic neared its end. According to the constitution, the Republic's first president could serve only two years and could not succeed himself. Sam Houston left office on December 1, 1838, succeeded by Mirabeau B. Lamar, who had based his election campaign on criticisms of Houston. Sam got even with Lamar at the inaugural ball. The new president planned to give a speech, which he had prepared for days. First, however, Sam Houston, as the outgoing president, rose to introduce the new president of the Republic. Dressed in knee britches with silver buckles, a silk coat, and a powdered wig, he talked for three hours. By the time Houston got through with his long-winded speech, Lamar was so upset he could not deliver his speech to the small number of people who remained in the audience.

In the spring of 1839, Sam Houston went to Mobile, Alabama, on business regarding the annexation of Texas and land development in the Republic. At a garden party, he met Margaret Moffette Lea. The forty-six-year-old Sam, and the poised twenty-year-old were immediately drawn to each other. Margaret's tall, slender figure, her shiny, wavy brown hair, and her expressive eyes captured Sam's heart. By the end of one week, they were talking about marriage as they gazed at a lone star in the southern sky. Sam called it the "star of destiny," and it became their special symbol.

Sam left Mobile and traveled to the Hermitage, where he visited the retired Andrew Jackson. From there he wrote to Margaret, asking her to marry him. Although she quickly accepted, Houston did not receive her answer for several weeks due to the slow mail delivery. Sam sent Margaret a cameo portrait of himself to symbolize their engagement, and Margaret wore it on a green ribbon around her neck. Margaret's family had concerns about the marriage because of the twenty-six-year age difference and stories they had heard about Houston's drinking. Even when Sam returned to Alabama in August to visit his fiancee, her family still hoped the marriage would not occur. When a friend asked Margaret why she had so quickly agreed to marriage to a man opposed by her family, Margaret replied, "He had won my heart."

Houston went back to Texas and learned of two events that had occurred during his absence. Voters in San Augustine had elected him to represent them in the Republic's fourth congress, which would convene in December 1839. He also discovered that President Lamar had moved the state capital from Houston to Austin.

Although twenty-six years her senior, Sam Houston married Margaret Moffet Lea in 1840. *(Courtesy of the University of Texas.)*

Houston opposed the move because he believed Austin was open to attack and that neither the archives nor the government officials would be safe there.

When Sam told his friends the news about his engagement, they tried to discourage the marriage. They remembered Sam's despair when his earlier marriage had failed and did not want to see him slip back into the misery of those days. From Texas, Sam wrote long love letters to Margaret. He had previously invited Margaret's mother, a clever businesswoman, to visit Texas to consider buying land there. Now he begged Margaret to come to Texas with her mother in February 1840, so that the couple could marry. Margaret agreed and told Sam on which ship they would arrive.

Despite their opposition to his marriage, some of Sam's friends decided to fire a cannon to welcome his bride-to-be when she arrived. The boom of the cannon frightened those on board because they thought their ship was under attack. Sam rowed out in a small boat to meet the ship, but Margaret was not on deck. Sam asked Mrs. Lea where Margaret was. Mrs. Lea replied: "General Houston, my daughter is in Alabama. She goes forth in the world to marry no man. The man who receives her hand will receive it in my home and not elsewhere."

After Mrs. Lea had invested in some Texas lands, she returned to Alabama, where she again tried to discourage Margaret from marrying Sam Houston. In Texas, Houston's friends continued to argue against the marriage as well. No one could discourage the couple, however, and Sam went back to Alabama to claim his bride. The wedding took place at the home of Henry Lea, Margaret's brother, on May 9, 1840, in Marion, Perry County, Alabama. For the wedding twenty-one-year-old Margaret had made her own trousseau—a white satin dress for the ceremony and two other dresses of purple silk and blue muslin. Sam gave Margaret a small gold wedding band because she preferred good quality plain jewelry. Houston, now forty-seven, finally had his heart's desire, his esperanza, "the one hoped for."

Margaret's strongest desire was that her new husband stop drinking. She had good cause for concern. This was the heaviest-drinking era in the nation's history. Americans at this time consumed an average of 7.1 gallons of liquor per year, and many believed drinking liquor was essential to a healthy diet. Margaret began her attempts to reform Sam while they were still on their honeymoon. She must have had some early success because when the couple stopped to visit in Sam's old hometown of Nacogdoches, Texas, Sam drank only water, much to everyone's surprise.

Sam and Margaret spent the early days of their marriage in San Augustine. But after Sam was re-elected to a seat in the Texas fifth congress on September 7, 1840, he and his bride moved to Houston. Margaret had trouble adjusting to the Texas climate and became quite ill. Finally, she went back to Alabama to get well. When she recovered, she returned to Texas, and the couple had their first home at Cedar Point in the Galveston Bay area. Margaret used her skills to turn the two-room house into a home.

While Sam Houston served in the Texas House of Representatives during Lamar's term of office, he continued to criticize the second president at every opportunity. Houston had good reason to do so. During his term as president, Lamar made decisions that drove Texas even deeper into conflict and debt. Because of his wars with the Indians, Lamar needed some quick cash for the state treasury. The Santa Fe Trail ran through part of what was considered Texas at that time. Lamar believed the residents of the New Mexico territory would rather be Texans than Mexicans, and he made a plan to bring about that change. If successful, Texas could collect taxes on all of the goods that made their way down the trail.

When the Texas congress turned down Lamar's proposal, he forged ahead on his own with the Santa Fe Expedition, which he called a trade mission. Texas merchants and government stores filled twenty-one large wagons with goods worth two hundred thousand dollars—a very large amount at that time. The Expedition left Austin on June 19, 1841. A lack of sufficient provisions and a mistake in identifying a river caused the wagon train to come to a halt, where it became easy prey for Comanche and Kiowa Indians. When the survivors reached New Mexico, the governor did not welcome them. Instead he took them prisoner and sent them to jail in Mexico City. Sam Houston's prediction to the Texas congress that no good would come of Lamar's plan proved true, and this gave Houston more ammunition to use against Lamar.

Another of Lamar's attempts to make money negatively affected Texas's relationship with Mexico and nearly destroyed the state's navy. Lamar had rented the Republic's navy to Mexican rebels based in Yucatan. Under the command of a thirty-year-old Virginian, Edwin W. Moore, the navy preyed on Mexican ships. Just two days before his term of office ended, Lamar signed an agreement with the Yucatan rebel chief to continue to supply the Texas naval ships for eight thousand dollars per month and half of whatever the rebels seized from the Mexican ships. This arrangement caused bitterness between Moore and Sam Houston and even threatened the navy's continued existence.

Since Lamar could not serve a second consecutive term, Houston decided to run again. He found himself in a nasty, mudslinging campaign against David Burnet, Lamar's vice-president, who challenged Houston to a duel. Houston declined, as he now did with all such challenges, and easily won the election on September 6, 1841, receiving 7,915 votes to Burnet's 3,619. Houston's running mate, Edward Burleson, defeated Memucan Hunt for vice-president, and their supporters gained control of congress. A huge crowd of people attended the victory dinner in Washington County, where they served thirteen barbecued hogs, two sides of beef roasted

The capital of Texas was relocated from Houston to Austin in 1839.
*(Courtesy of Texas State Archives.)*

with honey, potatoes, chickens, and pastries. At the celebration, Houston did not drink any alcohol, amazing those who knew about his previous drinking habits.

Sam Houston's second term as president began in December 1841. This time he had three major goals: to cut the cost of government and gain credit from other countries so that the Texas government could make purchases, to reverse the hostile policy against the Indians begun by Lamar, and to renew efforts to get Texas annexed by the United States. In addition, he had to deal with Mexico and Santa Anna, who had returned to power the same year that Houston was re-elected.

In March 1842, Santa Anna, who judged the Texas government's problems a sign of weakness, sent a small force to invade San Antonio, Goliad, and Refugio. Taking all three towns by surprise, the Mexicans captured and held each of the settlements for a few days. Many citizens, fearing this action was the beginning of a major Mexican invasion, fled to less populated towns. Sam Houston declared a state of emergency and sent a representative to the United States to seek help. Then he called a special session of the Texas congress; but by the time the lawmakers could gather, the invaders had gone back to Mexico. Although the Texas congress wanted to declare war on Mexico, Houston believed such an action would only unite Mexicans against Texans and vetoed the idea. Then on September 11, 1842, General Adrian Woll led a second surprise attack on San Antonio at night, in a dense fog. A cannon shot and military music from the public square awakened San Antonians the next morning. The Mexican army occupied the town for more than a week; and when they left, Woll's troops took with them a judge, a jury panel, and three lawyers. These actions renewed many Texans' desire to invade Mexico.

Sam Houston ordered two companies of militia, about twelve thousand men, to San Antonio and put General Alexander Somervell in charge of pursuing the Mexican army to the Rio Grande. Somervell moved slowly, and when he ordered a retreat near Gonzales, three hundred soldiers decided to ignore orders and marched instead toward the Rio Grande. They took the town of Mier before 176 of them were captured by the Mexican army and placed in prison. Santa Anna declared that one out of every ten soldiers would be shot. To determine the victims, he used a pot containing both black and white beans. The Mexicans executed the men who drew out the seventeen black beans. The rest of the Texans were not released from Perote Prison for several more years, and Houston again had to fight the pressure to attack Mexico. One reason Houston refused to get involved in an all-out war with Mexico was that he knew Texas did not have the resources to fight and win such a war.

Besides his unpopular stance on the situation with Mexico, Houston did not fare well in public opinion in regard to the state's capital either. Never having wanted Austin as the capital, he tried to compromise by relocating the government to Washington-on-the-Brazos. Many members of the seventh congress protested this move by arriving two months late for their legislative session. In order to be a complete capital, Washington-on-the-Brazos needed the republic's archives. Houston sent a small force of Texas rangers to Austin to retrieve the archives and bring them to a place of safety and convenience for conducting business.

The men loaded the documents on December 30, 1842, in preparation for their return. Just as the rangers started down Congress Avenue, Mrs. Angelina Eberly, a hotel manager, sounded an alarm by running out into the street and firing a cannon kept there in case of Indian attack. Although she did some damage to the General Land Office, the cannon roused a group of men to chase the archive wagons. The next morning, the

The Houston family moved to Raven Hill in 1845. *(Courtesy of the University of Texas.)*

men from Austin surrounded the archive wagons and forced the return of the records to Austin. Sam Houston had lost the "Archives War," but he refused to go to Austin as long as he was president of the Republic.

Another problem Sam faced was the need to restore good relations with the Indians. Mirabeau Lamar's administration had not treated them well, so Houston had to work to convince the Indians that a lasting peace was possible. He signed treaties with several tribes, agreeing to keep settlers off their lands if the Indians would remain on those lands and do their part to keep the peace. He also tried to insure that the traders would not cheat the Indians by allowing only the Torrey Trading Company to trade with the Indians. That company consistently gave the natives fair prices for their skins and other goods. Company representatives assured the Indian buyers that tools and goods they purchased were of good quality at fair prices. Throughout his second term, Houston had little trouble with the Indians.

When Houston began his second term as president, the Republic was close to financial failure. He lowered the cost of running the government to almost nothing by cutting salaries below the cost of living, providing no money for a regular army, and closing some government offices. Total government expenses during his second term were five hundred thousand dollars compared to about five million dollars spent during Lamar's presidency. Although the value of Texas money increased somewhat due to these actions, Houston knew Texas would go bankrupt if annexation did not happen soon.

At home, the Houstons welcomed their first child, Sam Jr., on May 25, 1843, just before the annexing of Texas became a major issue in the United States presidential election. Houston had hinted strongly to Congress that Texas and Great Britain were growing closer. Americans did not want a British presence on their continent, and President John Tyler promoted the annexation of Texas. Then in the next election, Democrat nominee James K. Polk supported taking Texas as another state. His victory made annexation more likely, and immigration to Texas increased, as did the value of Texas money and bonds.

In early 1845, the Houston family moved to their new farm, called Raven Hill, fifteen miles outside Huntsville, Texas. Although the house was a small, rough, log building, Margaret liked it because she thought Sam would now retire from politics to stay home with her. In June, Sam received word that his long-time mentor, Andrew Jackson, was dying. Sam took his two-year-old son, Sam Jr., and set out for the Hermitage, hoping the boy could meet this great man before he died. They arrived too late. When he learned that his friend had already died, Sam, loyal to the end, fell to his knees and sobbed his despair. Then he pulled his young son to him and said, "My son, try to remember that you have looked upon the face of Andrew Jackson."

Sam's second term as president ended shortly before the annexation of Texas as the twenty-eighth state of the United States of America on December 29, 1845. While he was in Tennessee, Houston had been approached about running for the United States Senate, representing Texas. On February 21, 1846, the Texas legislature elected Houston a United States senator by a large majority, beginning a senatorial career that would last until 1859.

# Chapter Seven

---

## The War with Mexico

Sam Houston served as president of the Republic of Texas against the backdrop of the early years of the United States' war with Mexico. At the Battle of San Jacinto, Sam Houston had taken Santa Anna prisoner. While held captive in Texas, Santa Anna secretly signed the Treaty of Velasco, which recognized both Texas's independence and the Rio Grande as the boundary of Texas. Although the Mexican congress refused to accept the treaty, the Republic of Texas operated as an independent country for almost ten years. The United States and several foreign countries recognized Texas's independence, but Mexico never did. When the United States offered to annex Texas as a state in 1845, Mexico threatened war.

After Texas's annexation, the United States government reacted to Mexico's threat of war by placing troops under General Zachary Taylor at Corpus Christi. Mexico agreed to discussions about a peaceful settlement, but they had concerns other than the annexation, including unpaid claims against the Mexican government by private United States citizens. By the time the United States representative got to Mexico for the talks, the Mexican government was in turmoil and no one would meet with him. With the coming to power of a new Mexican president, Mariano Paredes y Arrilaga, relations between Mexico and the United States worsened. General Taylor received orders to defend the Rio Grande. Not surprisingly, the Mexicans made threats and demanded withdrawal of United States troops.

General Taylor responded by asking the United States Navy to blockade the mouth of the Rio Grande. Throughout 1846, tension grew along the border as Mexico built its troops in Matamoras to six thousand. This was more than twice the number of soldiers commanded by General Taylor, but the United States troops had spent the same time building a stronghold at Port Isabel. After Mexican troops crossed the Rio Grande and ambushed some American soldiers, Congress declared war on Mexico.

The first major battle of the Mexican War occurred at Palo Alto on May 7, 1846. The Mexicans suffered heavy losses and had to withdraw. Eventually, the Mexican army was driven back to Matamoras, which Americans occupied on May 18. In one of his daily long letters to Margaret, living over one thousand miles away, Houston asked what she thought about his joining the Texas forces in the war against Mexico. On June 20,

1846, Margaret answered his letter, "I wish you to be governed entirely by your own judgment, and though the decision may bring misery upon me beyond description, I will try to bear it without a murmur." By now the Houstons had a second child, a daughter, Nancy Elizabeth, or Nanny, born on September 6, 1846.

Sam Houston did not join the troops in Mexico. In September, a large American force attacked Monterey. The fighting was fierce, but the United States Army won. Two other forces mobilized in the next few months to march to Chihuahua. Sam continued to serve in Washington, where he looked forward to letters from his wife. Although Margaret wrote frequently, she failed to tell Sam about her health problems. For some time she

General Zachary Taylor led American troops during the Mexican-American War.
*(Courtesy of the Library of Congress.)*

had endured a painful lump in her right breast, but the family doctor, Ashbel Smith, had decided not to remove it until the breast no longer contained milk from the birth of her last child. In February 1847, the tumor burst, causing Margaret great pain. She called Dr. Smith, who operated to remove the pieces of the tumor. Margaret was so opposed to drinking liquor of any kind that she refused brandy as anesthesia, choosing instead to clinch her teeth on a silver dollar.

Someone else in Texas notified Sam about his wife's illness. He did not know its seriousness because Margaret had written only that she had been ill for ten to twelve days but was now strong enough to sit up and write to him. Upon receiving the news, Sam immediately left Washington, arriving at Raven Hill during the third week of March. For a while, Houston cared for his wife and children, and oversaw work on the farm. While Sam was in Texas, General Winfield Scott's army landed at Vera Cruz on its way to capture the capital, Mexico City. The United States Navy set up a blockade of the entire Mexican Gulf Coast. The only ship they allowed through was one carrying Sam Houston's old enemy, Santa Anna.

As it turned out, the "retirement" forced on Santa Anna by President Jackson after his defeat by Houston had not lasted long. France gave him another opportunity for military adventure when the French navy seized Vera Cruz in 1838. The French government sought indemnity for injuries to French citizens in Mexico. Santa

Anna led an army to Vera Cruz, where the French quickly set sail from their recent conquest. Once again, Santa Anna's exploits gained him the prestige to seize power. He led a revolt and established himself as dictator, ruling until he was again driven into exile in 1845.

The Mexican general owed his liberty and free passage through the U.S. Navy blockade to President Polk. Santa Anna had persuaded the president to let him come out of exile in Cuba to lead a Mexican peace party. Of course, he had lied to Polk about the attempt to work for peace. Instead he began to build an army of twenty-five thousand Mexican soldiers to attack General Scott.

Sam Houston, meanwhile, worried about his wife, not about Santa Anna. Margaret did not seem to get better. The stitches bothered her, and she believed she

James K. Polk served as president of the United States during the Mexican-American War. *(Courtesy of the Library of Congress.)*

had found another tumor in her breast. In April, Houston again sent for Dr. Smith, who assured them the healing was progressing normally and there was no new tumor. As soon as Houston heard the doctor's verdict, he began to think about returning to Washington. His first term as senator was drawing to a close, and he wanted to run again. He started to travel the state to gain votes, and at the end of the year, voters returned him to Washington for another term. As he headed toward the nation's capital, he left behind a wife pregnant with their third child.

In Mexico, Vera Cruz fell to American troops on March 29, 1847. General Scott left a small force to guard the city and marched his remaining troops toward Mexico City. After several delays waiting for replacements of troops whose volunteer terms had ended, Scott's forces were strong enough to advance on Mexico City in August. Santa Anna led the defense of that city, but the Mexicans could not stop the Americans. In September, United States Marines took over the National Palace, the "Halls of Montezuma," and raised the American flag.

In Washington, Houston learned about the progress of the Mexican War as well as about America's drive to take New Mexico and California. In 1846, the United States claimed that as a part of its annexation of Texas, it was also entitled to what is the eastern half of present-day New Mexico. The government sent Colonel Stephen Watts Kearney to lay claim to this territory. He had a dual mission: secure New Mexico and then press on to California.

Kearney and his troops followed the Santa Fe Trail across the vast plains. Kearney hoped for a bloodless takeover of New Mexico, but the governor of New Mexico, General Manuel Armijo, vowed to give his life to defend his country. That first night, Armijo held a secret meeting with American representatives. On August 18, 1846, the American troops rode into Santa Fe unopposed. Armijo and his army had disappeared! Kearney left some soldiers behind to protect Santa Fe, and he, along with three hundred dragoons, set out for California. Although some natives later attempted an uprising, it was stopped. By January 1847, New Mexico was secure and quiet.

Other Americans had already staked claims to Upper California before Kearney arrived. Among these early settlers was Lt. Colonel John Fremont. Frontier scout Kit Carson told Kearney that Upper California was already in United States' hands, but Kearney continued his march westward. At that time, Commodore Robert F. Stockton, a naval commander, was in charge of Los Angeles, but rebels surprised the town in October 1846, and the Americans had to withdraw. The United States' attempts to retake the town were unsuccessful.

Kearney and his exhausted men arrived in California in late 1846. After they had time to recover, Kearney met with Stockton to plan a joint navy-army attack on Los Angeles. On January 10, 1847, they retook the town. Lt. Colonel Fremont negotiated the peace treaty. The navy now shifted its focus to Baja California. On April 14, 1847, they occupied the port of La Paz. They also attacked the west coast cities of Guaymas and Mazatlan. When peace negotiations began with Mexico, Baja California became an issue. The Mexican government absolutely refused to give up that piece of land. To bring the negotiations to a close, the United States agreed to let Mexico keep Baja California and paid them fifteen million dollars for New Mexico and Upper California. A newspaper correspondent carried the signed Treaty of Guadalupe Hidalgo from Mexico City to Washington, D.C., and delivered it to President James Polk on February 19, 1848.

Because not everyone in the United States agreed with the expansion, Sam Houston left his duties in the Senate in February to go on a speaking tour in support of westward movement. He said, "There is an instinct in the American people which impels them onward, which will lead them to pervade this continent, to develop its resources, to civilize its people, and receive the rich bounties of the creating power of divine Providence." Because he was not in Washington, he was unaware that the treaty had already been signed.

While negotiators had worked out the treaty, gold was found on John A. Sutter's place on the American River in California. Word of the discovery of gold did not spread before Mexico and the United States had signed the treaty. Had Mexico known of the rich bounty

Following the discovery of gold at Sutters Mill, Americans flocked to California in 1848.

in California, it might have refused the treaty. But it did sign, and by May 1848, Americans had flocked to California. On July 4 of that year, President Polk finally told the American people about the treaty. After seventeen months of combat, the War with Mexico had ended, and the nation's boundary stretched to the Pacific Ocean. But the spoils of war—an additional one-half million square miles of land in the new territories—would bring to a head the issue of slavery.

While he was busy with his obligations as a United

States senator, Sam often felt guilty about the time he spent away from Margaret and their children. He knew that Margaret wanted him to convert to the Baptist religion. Because of her encouragement, and perhaps to clear his conscience about leaving her so often, Sam attended the E Street Baptist Church in Washington from time to time. Whenever he went to a service, he wrote Margaret his impressions. He probably did not share with her the fact that throughout the service, he whittled toys for the children at church, leaving behind a pile of wood shavings for the custodian to pick up.

Sam had his eye on the U.S. presidential election of 1852, and by 1848, he had almost stopped attending church in order to travel throughout the country to give speeches. He was not at home on April 13, when Margaret gave birth to their second daughter, Margaret Lea. Before long, Sam returned home long enough to move the family from Raven Hill to a less isolated home on the edge of Huntsville, Texas.

Sam had returned to Washington by the time Margaret's troubles developed with Virginia Thorne, a ward of the Houstons. Margaret's sister had earlier adopted the girl, an orphan. When Margaret's sister died, the Houstons took the girl in and she worked as a servant in the household. As she grew older, she started to resent her servant role. Problems developed between her and Margaret, and the girl started spending time with the farm's overseer, Thomas Gott. She had convinced him that she was nineteen instead of fourteen.

Nanny, Mary Willie, and Maggie Houston were three of Sam and Margaret's
eight children. *(Courtesy of the Library of Congress.)*

One night, as Margaret and Virginia tried to put little
Sam and Nanny to bed, Nanny resisted. Virginia became upset with the child and jerked her out of the bed
to the floor. She then dragged the crying child to Margaret, who kept yelling at Virginia not to hurt Nanny.
The angry Margaret whipped Virginia with a cowhide
strip that drew blood on her shoulders, back and arms.
After this incident, Virginia eloped with the overseer,
who had himself appointed the girl's guardian. Gott
encouraged Virginia to file charges that Mrs. Houston
had abused her. Later that year, Margaret was charged
with assault and battery against the girl.

Back in Washington, senators argued over the slavery issue. California had applied for statehood. If California came in as a free state, the balance of power in the Senate would shift to the free states. The Southern states, which held a one-vote majority in the Senate, started to talk about secession. Sam Houston made it clear he believed the Union must be preserved. While others wanted to divide the nation, he wanted to keep it whole. Houston believed his strong opinions held the government together in this time of crisis. He wrote long, loving letters to Margaret, saying the reason he did not come home to see her and the children was that the government would not function in his absence.

Although the United States was at peace along all of its borders in 1850, Americans became their own enemies over whether new states admitted to the Union should be slave states or free. Houston introduced a resolution in the Senate that Congress should not have any power over whether a state had slavery or not. He believed the voters of each state should decide such an issue. His resolution led to Henry Clay's Compromise of 1850. This compromise provided for California's admission as a free state, with the other property gained from Mexico becoming the territories of New Mexico and Utah. The people of these territories would decide the slavery issue for themselves. To appease the Southerners, the compromise included the Fugitive Slave Law. This law required people in free states to help catch and return escaped slaves.

Few people liked the compromise. Southerners resented the admission of California as a free state, and threats to secede surfaced again. Northerners, who had supported the Underground Railroad to help escaped slaves make their way northward, hated the Fugitive Slave Act. In a stirring speech on February 8, Sam Houston told Congress, "A nation divided against itself cannot stand." Both sides decided to give the compromise a chance.

Because Houston focused so much of his time on the anti-slavery issue rather than on other issues important to the South, resentment against him developed in that region, though his popularity grew in the North and the West. Then, without telling anyone his reasons, Sam abruptly left Washington in late February to go home. He had heard about the charges against his wife.

Sam arrived in Texas in early March and hired Henderson Yoakum to defend Margaret, but the preliminary hearing was postponed because Margaret was about to give birth to their fourth child, Mary Willie. By the time the baby arrived on April 9, 1850, Sam had returned to Washington. When the jury finally heard the case, they deadlocked in a tie vote. This allowed the case to go to the local Baptist church, where the elders decided Margaret's fate. Because of her strong faith and her many activities in the church, the elders found Margaret "not guilty." In later years the Houstons learned that some of Sam Houston's political enemies had encouraged the accusations against Margaret.

In Washington, Sam spoke out in defense of the

Union every chance that he got. He continued his preference for flashy dress, wearing several large rings and a large gold pocket watch, and carrying a gold-headed cane and gold-encased pencil. By 1851, many began to see him as the front runner for the Democratic nomination for president. Sam, however, never said whether or not he planned to run, and the time for him to become a contender came and went.

For the next two years, Sam removed himself from the public eye. Margaret gave birth to their fourth daughter, Antoinette Power, on June 20, 1852, and in September 1853, Houston bought two hundred wooded acres of farmland at Independence, Texas. Sam Jr., enrolled in Baylor University. In Washington, the slavery issue again resurfaced in Congress in 1854 as a result of a proposed transcontinental railroad. Stephen Douglas, a powerful senator from Illinois, wanted to create two new territories, Kansas and Nebraska, so that the railroad would not to have to cross such a vast undeveloped area. Since both states were north of the latitude established by the Missouri Compromise of 1820, they should have automatically been free states.

Douglas, however, needed to win Southern support, so he proposed doing away with the Missouri Compromise and letting the people in each territory decide the slavery issue. His idea, known as the Kansas-Nebraska Act, passed with the solid backing of the South, except for Sam Houston, who begged his fellow lawmakers not to reopen old wounds over slavery. Although he knew he had little chance of stopping the bill and realized his vote against it would perhaps ruin his political future, Houston did not hesitate. He was one Southern Democrat who believed in the Union more than the South. The Texas State Convention attacked his vote, and the Dallas *Herald* demanded he resign his Senate seat. Sam replied, "I know neither North nor South, I know only the Union."

Despite these attacks from the South, Sam again started to look at the presidency, supported by people from the North and the West. He made speeches throughout the country and was seldom at home. He even missed the birth of his second son, Andrew Jackson Houston, on June 21, 1854. The family in Independence needed him. Margaret and the children wanted their husband and father at home.

Sam Houston's gratitude for another son did bring about his joining the Baptist church as a reflection of his belief in the power of prayer. The night before the baptism, vandals destroyed the church's coffin-shaped baptismal font. Margaret's minister, the Reverend Rufus Burleson, had to baptize Sam in the icy waters of Rocky Creek near Independence on November 19, 1854. A few days later, an incident with a young black boy demonstrated that Sam took his conversion vows seriously.

While driving into Huntsville, Houston noticed a crowd gathered in front of the general store. To satisfy his curiosity, he walked over to see what was happening. He saw that a slave owner, noted for his meanness and harsh temper, was auctioning off a black boy. The boy was very small from the mistreatment he had endured, and because of this, people believed the owner when he claimed the boy was eight years old.

Sam Houston called out to the slave owner and asked what kind of bids he had for the boy. The slave owner said that he had an offer of five hundred dollars, but the bidder had gone home to get the money. Sam Houston offered $450 cash to the slave owner right then. Houston walked over to the boy and told him not to be frightened anymore. He said he was taking the boy, Jeff Hamilton, home with him to become a playmate for his son. At home, Houston treated Jeff like one of his own children, giving him chores to do and disciplining him when necessary. Jeff lived to the age of 110 years.

Ironically, his split with many Texans over the slavery issue caused the state legislature to inform Houston they would not return him to the Senate when his term expired in 1859. Just as the Senate adjourned, the courts handed down the Dred Scott decision on March 6, 1857. This ruling stated that a slave did not become free when taken to a free territory, that Congress could not prevent a territory from having slavery, and that blacks could not be citizens. That decision opened the entire West to slavery and increased the conflict between North and South, moving the country closer to the Civil War.

Houston traveled home during the congressional recess and in May learned that the Democratic convention had nominated Lieutenant Governor Hardin R. Runnels for governor of Texas. Runnels was a strong supporter of a state's right to secede from the Union. Sam Houston decided to run against him. Campaigning as an independent, with no political party and no newspaper supporting him, Sam traveled across the state in a red buggy with large gold lettering. He wore an old, loose linen coat to protect his clothes from the dust. He used a large turkey feather fan to keep cool and to fight off the flies as he delivered sixty-seven speeches in two months. Sometimes, when it got too hot as he spoke, Sam would take off his shirt and bare his chest and his war wounds.

Houston endured constant belittling and even threats of tarring and feathering for his talk about preserving the Union. He had little chance against the organization supporting Runnels, but still ran a remarkably close race, receiving 28,678 votes to Runnels's 32,552 in the August election. For the first time, Texans failed to elect Houston to an office he had campaigned for. Despite the defeat, Houston did not bow to pressure to resign his Senate seat and returned to Washington in November for the opening of the thirty-fifth Congress.

# Chapter Eight

## Texas and Secession

Filled with energy from the governor's race in spite of his loss, Sam Houston resumed his duties as senator from Texas. He was sixty-five years old. Back in Texas, Margaret gave birth to their seventh child, William Rogers, on May 25, 1858. Sam wrote to his wife often and seemed to look forward to spending more time with his family. He spent the summer on a speaking tour, causing many to believe he did not intend to retire. Houston frequently addressed the Senate in his last months as a member of that body. His main theme was always his belief in the Union. In his final speech to the senators, he announced he would be proud to have this epitaph on his tombstone: "He loved his country, he was a patriot; he was devoted to the Union."

When he returned home, Houston was disturbed to hear the talk about Texas seceding from the United States. Sam Houston strongly opposed secession and in 1859 got involved in the governor's race again, thinking he could prevent Texas from leaving the Union. His opponent was current Governor Hardin Runnels, the Democratic nominee. Again Sam Houston had no party affiliation and no campaign fund. In contrast to the race two years earlier, Houston did little traveling. He made one speech in Nacogdoches, Texas, on July 9, 1859. He appealed to the voters to support the Union and to avoid secession, telling them: "Preserve Union and you preserve Liberty. They are one and the same, indivisible and perfect."

Most of the state's powerful newspapers attacked him for his Union stand. Regardless of this, the election results were different this time around, and Houston won by about the same margin he had lost by two years earlier. With his 33,375 votes to Runnels's 27,500 votes, Sam Houston became the only man to serve as governor of two different states. Houston ignored tradition and delivered his inaugural address directly to the people from the steps of the Capitol instead of before a joint session of the legislature. He told the people he was a governor of the people, not of a party.

The Houstons moved into the Governor's Mansion in Austin, where Margaret had their eighth child, Temple Lea, on August 12, 1860. Houston had been in office only one month when the South Carolina legislature passed a resolution that any state had the right to secede. When Houston received the resolution, he sent it to the Texas legislature with a strong recommendation not to pass it. Through some clever maneuvers, the pro-

Houston minorities in both houses managed to keep the South Carolina resolution from passing.

But the main issue was not dead. The national presidential election would either calm or excite Southern leaders. When Abraham Lincoln won the election by a narrow margin, South Carolina took the lead in calling for a secession convention. Five other Southern governors and almost all of the senators and representatives from the South had threatened secession if Lincoln won the election. After South Carolina voted to secede, Mississippi, Florida, Alabama, and Georgia quickly followed. Worried Texans sent petitions to Houston to demand that he call a convention for Texas to vote on seceding. Only the governor could call a convention when the legislature was not in session.

At first, Houston ignored the petitions, hoping the strong emotions would settle. Some of the local governments went ahead and elected delegates to a convention that had not been called. When it appeared that Texans would have a convention, even if illegally, Houston called a special session of the legislature to explain his position. He stated: "When Texas united her destiny with that of the United States, she entered not into the North or South; her connection was not sectional, but national." The legislators ignored his words. They wanted a convention and adjourned themselves.

The Secession Convention met on January 28, 1861, and elected Judge O.M. Roberts as its chairman. On February 1, tension grew as the roll call of the 174

Following the election of Abrahm Lincoln as president of the United States, Southern slave states began seceeding from the Union. *(Courtesy of the Library of Congress.)*

delegates began. Seventy men voted "for" secession before the first "no" vote was cast. The final count was 166 to 8 for immediate secession. A group of women walked to the platform and unfurled the Lone Star flag as the crowd cheered and applauded. Houston pled with the convention to let the people decide the issue of secession. He promised to make no speeches to try to sway the vote. He left the room without further speech. He was already sad for the future he foresaw for Texas and for the South.

On March 2, 1861, twenty-five years after its first declaration of independence, Texas left the Union. It was Sam Houston's sixty-eighth birthday. News reached Texas that Jefferson Davis of Mississippi had been chosen provisional president of the Confederate States of America. Georgia, Florida, and Louisiana had already seized federal property in their states, and a ship entering the Charleston, Virginia, harbor at Fort Sumter had been fired on.

The Texas secessionists did not wait for the results of the popular vote and started to take over federal property in Texas. On March 3, the popular tally was completed. Sam Houston was at home when he heard bells ringing and cannons booming. The citizens voted 46,129 in favor of secession with only 14,697 against it. When Sam heard the results of the people's vote, his face paled and the cords in his neck stood out. He told Margaret, "Texas is lost."

Houston tried to stop the alliance with the Confed-

Jefferson Davis was elected provisional president of the Confederate States of America on February 22, 1861. *(Courtesy of the Library of Congress.)*

eracy, claiming that the people had voted only for secession, not for joining the Confederacy. No one paid any attention to his argument, and the convention delegates voted 109 to 2 that all state officers must take an oath of allegiance to the Confederacy or be removed from office. Sam Houston now had to make two big political decisions: whether to take the oath of allegiance and whether to fight to continue as governor. While wanting to stick to his principles, he feared for his family's safety. He had the power to maintain his position as governor and to prevent Texas's secession.

President Abraham Lincoln offered Sam the use of fifty thousand soldiers and the rank of major general as their commander to keep Texas in the Union.

Although Houston loved the Union, he loved Texas more and decided to yield to the convention's actions. Before noon on March 16, the day to take the oath, the presiding officer of the convention called Sam Houston's name three times. Houston was not there to respond. Instead, he was on the other side of the Governor's Mansion, writing his last message to the people as governor. Houston wrote: "I refuse to take this oath . . . In the name of my own conscience and my own manhood . . . I love Texas too well to bring civil strife and bloodshed upon her . . . [But] I will not yield those principles which I have fought for and struggled to maintain. The severest pang is that the blow comes in the name of the state of Texas. "

When Sam Houston did not appear, the convention unanimously declared the office of governor of Texas vacant and gave Lieutenant Governor Edward Clark temporary authority as governor. In a further vengeful act, the delegates gave the Houston family only twenty-four hours to vacate the Governor's Mansion. Sam and Margaret rented a house in Huntsville, Texas, called the Steamboat House because it looked so much like a riverboat. This was Houston's last residence. Some said Houston was never the same after these tumultuous events. He had stood by his principles, and now once again faced the darkest despair because of it.

Sam Jr. was wounded and left for dead at the Battle of Shiloh.
*(Courtesy of the Library of Congress.)*

To add to Sam's distress, his eighteen-year-old son, Sam Jr., wanted to fight for the South. Sam tried to keep his oldest son busy with chores at their summer home, Cedar Point, giving him advice about plowing, planting, and building animal pens. At the same time, he urged Sam Jr. to wait to serve in the military until he could do so as a Texan rather than as a Confederate. Houston still hoped Texas would survive as an independent nation. But just as Sam had ignored his family years earlier to fight in the War of 1812, Sam Jr., now ignored his father's advice and begged for permission to join a group training at nearby Galveston. Sam Houston consented and even bought his son a Confederate uniform. His distressed mother gave her oldest son a small Bible.

From time to time, Houston visited Galveston, where his son was in training. When a colonel invited Sam to review the regiment, Houston wore his torn San Jacinto uniform. He tied his battered sword to his belt with the same buckskin thong he had used at San Jacinto. Sam threw down his gold-headed cane, walked unsteadily in front of the regiment, and yelled in his loudest voice that while the sons of several prominent people were not there, Sam Houston's son was present among the recruits to fight for the South.

On April 7, 1862, the Houstons received word that Sam Jr., had been wounded at Shiloh, but only later did they learn the circumstances of that day. Because of their success against the North on the previous day, Sam Jr.'s regiment approached their next battle with confidence. For some time, they could no see no sign of the Yankees. Suddenly, a fence ahead became a wall of fire, and Yankee soldiers swarmed the Confederates. Struck in the groin with a musket ball, Sam Jr. fell to the ground. As he went in and out of consciousness, he thought about his family back at Cedar Point. He wished he could see all of them before he died. A surgeon walked by Sam Jr. lying in the field in a pool of blood, but passed him up as one beyond help.

Later that afternoon, a Yankee chaplain noticed a slight movement in one of the bodies on the field. He knelt beside Sam Jr. and picked up a small Bible that

Sam Houston retired from public life following Texas's secession from the Union.
*(Courtesy of the University of Texas Library.)*

had fallen from the soldier's knapsack. He opened the Bible and read: "Sam Houston, Jr., from his mother, March 6, 1862." The chaplain asked Sam Jr. if he was related to General Houston of Texas who had served in the United States Senate. Sam Jr. weakly replied that the general was his father.

The chaplain had worked in the Senate during the time Houston served there, and he remembered Houston's speaking in favor of allowing ministers to petition the Senate. The chaplain jumped up, ran across the field, and returned with a surgeon. When the doctor discovered that Sam did not have a severed artery and that his blood had already started to coagulate, he told the chaplain to go find a litter to carry Sam Jr. off the field. Southern newspapers reported Sam Jr. as among the dead or missing, and Company C removed his name from their rolls.

While the Houstons hoped and prayed, they heard that a letter from another Confederate soldier revealed Sam Jr.'s imprisonment at Camp Douglas in St. Louis. Sam's parents held on to the hope that their son was still alive. In September 1862, a stranger walked up to their house. Pale and wearing ragged clothes, he leaned on two crutches made of saplings. His own brothers and sisters playing outside did not recognize the man with sunken eyes, skin pulled tight over his cheeks, and long hair hanging over his collar. But his mother knew Sam Jr., and she threw her arms around him, breaking into sobs as she hugged him. After a bath and some rest, Sam Jr., told his family about his experience at Shiloh, and the chaplain who had saved him on the battlefield.

Sam Houston spent the days of the Civil War sitting under a huge oak tree and smoking his pipe. With a blue velvet hat to protect his balding head, and soft, yellow moccasins on his feet, he kept the leg he had injured at San Jacinto propped on a stool. Although opposed to secession, he had given his oldest son to fight for the South. He still yearned for an independent Texas. In the war between the North and the South, he feared for the

South. When he heard Vicksburg and Gettysburg had both fallen to Yankee troops on July 7, Sam developed a cold and fever that turned into pneumonia. He had received a deathblow when Texas seceded from the Union and was hit by a second one with the Confederate defeats. For three weeks he was confined to his bed before he went into a coma. No one could awaken him, but the next afternoon they heard his feeble voice saying, "Texas! Texas!" As Margaret sat by his side and held his hand, his lips moved one more time to whisper, "Margaret." Then he spoke no more.

Death came for Houston at sunset on July 16, 1863. He still wore on his finger the ring, inscribed with the word "Honor," given to him by his mother more than fifty years earlier. On a rainy day, Margaret buried her beloved Sam in Huntsville's Oakwood Cemetery. At his grave, the family placed a plain slab with Sam's name and dates of birth and death. Today, a twenty-five foot shaft of gray Texas granite bearing Andrew Jackson's words, "The world will take care of Houston's fame," rises above his burial plot. After Houston's death, Margaret moved back to Independence with her eight children, the youngest one only three years old. She died four years later, in 1867, of yellow fever.

To know Sam Houston's life is to follow the progress of the United States from just after the American Revolution to the Civil War. His life spanned the United States' dealings with the Indians, westward expansion, slavery, and secession. He personally knew thirteen of the first fifteen presidents of the United States. Houston held more military and political offices than anyone else in American history. In the military, he served as a United States army lieutenant and a major general in both the Tennessee militia and the Republic of Texas army. After he settled in Texas, he chaired two committees that wrote constitutions to craft Texas's independence. In Tennessee, he was a district attorney, a congressional representative, and governor of that state. Texans twice elected him president of the Republic, sent him to Washington as a senator for thirteen years, and elected him governor of the state of Texas.

Today his name can be found throughout Texas—as one of the largest cities in the United States, on a university, at an army fort, on parks, and on numerous public schools. Just north of Lexington, Virginia, stands a large pink granite stone to mark his birthplace. The marker contains a tablet with a brief biography, the state seals of Texas, Virginia, and Tennessee, as well as the seals of the United States of America, the Cherokee Nation, and the Republic of Texas. Twenty miles southeast of Houston, Texas, the great San Jacinto monument rises 570 feet to commemorate the battle in which Houston led his army to achieve Texas's independence. To capture the true essence of this great and complex man is difficult. Perhaps he did as good a job as any when he described the kind of man needed to lead the Republic of Texas: "Brave enough for any trial, wise enough for any emergency, and cool enough for any crisis." Sam Houston was that kind of man.

# Timeline

1793 Sam Houston is born on March 2.

1806 Houston's father dies; family moves to Tennessee.

1809 Houston lives with Cherokee Indians.

1810 Cherokee Chief John Jolly adopts Houston.

1816 Elected to the U.S. House of Representatives from Tennessee.

1827 Becomes governor of Tennessee.

1829 Marries Eliza Allen; they separate several months later.

1835 Named commander-in-chief of East Texas army; elected major-general of army.

1836 Defeats Santa Anna's Mexican army; elected first president of the Republic of Texas.

1839 Elected member of Texas Congress.

1840 Weds Margaret Lea on May 9; reelected to Texas Congress.

1841 Takes oath of office for second term as President of Republic of Texas.

1846 Houston selected by Texas legislature as United States Senator from Texas.

1859 Elected governor of Texas for second time.

1863 Houston dies on July 16.

# Sources

## CHAPTER ONE: Early Years

p. 11, "My wigwam is yours . . ." Jack Gregory and Rennard Strickland, *Sam Houston with the Cherokees, 1829-1833* (Norman: University of Oklahoma Press, 1995), 10.

p. 19, "he preferred measuring . . ." C. Edwards Lester, *Life and Achievements of Sam Houston, Hero and Statesman* (New York: Hurst and Company, 1883), 17.

p. 25, "experienced a higher feeling . . ." George Creel, *Sam Houston: Colossus in Buckskin* (New York: Cosmopolitan Book Corporation, 1928), 10.

## CHAPTER TWO: Houston's Early Military Career

p. 27, "Remember . . . that while the door . . ." Lester, *Life and Achievements,* 21.

p. 32, "The sun was going . . ." Donald Day and Harry Herbert Ullom, eds. *The Autobiography of Sam Houston* (Norman: University of Oklahoma Press, 1954), 12.

p. 33, "Don't you know..." M.L. Wisehart, *Sam Houston: American Giant* (Washington: Robert B. Luce, Inc., 1962), 19.

p. 33, "When I reached . . ." Day and Ullom, eds. *The Autobiography of Sam Houston,* 14.

## CHAPTER THREE: From Leader to Outcast

p. 44, "I have no objection . . ." Henry Bruce, *Life of General Houston 1793-1863* (New York: Dodd, Mead, and Company, 1891), 77.

p. 48, "I wish they would . . ." Marquis James, *The Raven: A Biography of Sam Houston* (Austin: University of Texas Press, 1929), 117.

p. 49, "This is a painful . . ." Bruce, *General Houston 1793-1863*, 45.

p. 49, "I was in an agony . . ." Wisehart, *Sam Houston: American Giant*, 50.

p. 50, "Is the man mad?" Marshall DeBruhl, *Sword of San Jacinto: A Life of Sam Houston* (New York: Random House, 1993), 107.

p. 54, "A man who is drunk . . ." Wisehart, *Sam Houston: American Giant*, 62.

## CHAPTER FOUR: The Pendulum Swings

p. 55, "So he doesn't know . . ." Creel, *Sam Houston: Colossus in Buckskin*, 52.

p. 56, "Meaner than I ever felt . . ." Wisehart, *Sam Houston: American Giant*, 68.

p. 59, "I am tired . . ." Bruce, *General Houston 1793-1863*, 75.

p. 60, "I except [sic] your gift . . ." James, *The Raven: A Biography of Sam Houston*, 186.

p. 65, "the finest country . . ." Bruce, *Life of General Houston 1793-1863*, 82.

p. 65, "It is probable that . . ." Amelia W. Williams and Eugene C. Barker, eds. *The Writings of Sam Houston,* I (Austin: Pemberton Press, 1970), 276.

## CHAPTER FIVE: Call to War

p. 68, "War is our only . . ." Alfred M. Williams, *Sam Houston and the War of Independence in Texas* (Boston: Houghton, Mifflin, and Company), 94.

p. 70, "Who will go with . . ." Ibid., 109.

p. 72, "I have ordered . . ." Williams and Barker, eds. *The Writings of Sam Houston*, I, 339.

p. 78, "If only three hundred . . ." James, *The Raven: A Biography of Sam Houston*, 232.

p. 78, "The enemy are laughing . . ." Clifford Hopewell, *Sam Houston: Man of Destiny* (Austin: Eakin Press, 1987), 195.

p. 81, "This morning we are..." Williams and Barker, eds., *The Writings of Sam Houston*, I, 413.

p. 83, "To Miss Anna Raguet..." James, *The Raven: A Biography of Sam Houston*, 253.

## CHAPTER SIX: Leader of Texas

p. 91, "You shall remain..." *About North Georgia*, http://ngeorgia.com/history/cherokeeforts.html, 1994-2000.

p. 93, "He had won my heart." James, *The Raven: A Biography of Sam Houston*, 309.

p. 95, "General Houston, my daughter . . ." Ibid., 313.

p. 104, "My son, try to remember . . ." Wisehart, *Sam Houston: American Giant*, 484.

## CHAPTER SEVEN: The War with Mexico

p. 107, "I wish you to be . . ." Llerena Friend, *Sam Houston: The Great Designer* (Austin: University of Texas Press, 1954), 176.

p. 112, "There is an instinct . . ." Williams and Barkers, eds., *The Writings of Sam Houston*, V, 34.

p. 117, "A nation divided . . ." Ibid., 144.

p. 119, "I know neither North . . ." John F. Kennedy, *Profiles in Courage* (New York: Harper & Row, Publishers, 1964), 92.

## CHAPTER EIGHT: Texas and Secession

p. 122, "He loved his country . . ." Williams and Barker, eds., *The Writings of Sam Houston,* VII, 205.

p. 123, "Preserve Union . . ." Wisehart, *Sam Houston: American Giant,* 582.

p. 124, "When Texas united . . ." John F. Kennedy, *Sam Houston and the Senate* (Austin: The Pemberton Press, 1970), 23.

p. 126, "Texas is lost." Bruce, *Life of General Houston, 1793-1863,* 215.

p. 128, "I refuse to take . . ." Williams and Barker, eds., *The Writings of Sam Houston,* VIII, 277.

p. 133, "Texas . . ." DeBruhl, *Sword of San Jacinto: A Life of Sam Houston,* 402.

p. 133, "Margaret." Ibid.

p. 133, "The world will take care . . ." Lester, *Life and Achievements of Sam Houston, Hero and Statesman,* 157.

p. 134, "Brave enough for any trial . . ." Wisehart, *Sam Houston: American Giant,* 648.

# Bibliography

Bruce, Henry. *Life of General Houston 1793-1863*. New York: Dodd, Mead, and Company, 1993.

Campbell, Randolph B. *Sam Houston and the American Southwest*. New York: Harper Collins Publishers, 1993.

Creel, George. *Sam Houston: Colossus in Buckskin*. New York: Cosmopolitan Book Corporation, 1928.

Day, Donald, and Harry Herbert Ullom, eds. *The Autobiography of Sam Houston*. Norman: University of Oklahoma Press, 1954.

DeBruhl, Marshall. *Sword of San Jacinto: A Life of Sam Houston*. New York: Random House, 1993.

Friend, Llerena. *Sam Houston: The Great Designer*. Austin: University of Texas Press, 1954.

Gregory, Jack, and Rennard Strickland. *Sam Houston with the Cherokees, 1829-1833*. Norman: University of Oklahoma Press, 1995.

Hopewell, Clifford. *Sam Houston: Man of Destiny*. Austin: Eakin Press, 1987.

James, Marquis. *The Raven: A Biography of Sam Houston*. Austin: University of Texas Press, 1929.

Kennedy, John F. *Profiles in Courage*. Memorial Edition. New York: Harper & Row, Publishers, 1964.

Kennedy, John F. *Sam Houston and the Senate.* Austin: The Pemberton Press, 1970.

Lester, C. Edwards. *Life and Achievements of Sam Houston, Hero and Statesman.* New York: Hurst and Company, 1883.

McDowell, Bart. "Sam Houston: A Man Too Big for Texas." *National Geographic* 169, no. 3 (March 1986): 311-329.

Peacock, Howard. "Sam Houston, Texas Hero." *Texas Highways* 40, no. 3 (March 1993): 4-13.

Williams, Alfred M. *Sam Houston and the War of Independence in Texas.* Boston: Houghton, Mifflin and Company, 1895.

Williams, Amelia W. and Eugene C. Barkers, eds. *The Writings of Sam Houston*, 8 vols. Austin: Pemberton Press, 1970.

Williams, John Hoyt. *Sam Houston: A Biography of the Father of Texas.* New York: Simon & Schuster, 1993.

Wisehart, M. K. *Sam Houston: American Giant.* Washington: Robert B Luce, Inc., 1962.

**Websites**
*Trail of Tears*
   http://ngeorgia.com/history/cherokeeforts.html
*Sam Houston Memorial Museum*
   http://www.shsu.edu/~smm_www/
*The Handbook of Texas Online*
   http://www.tsha.utexas.edu/handbook/online/articles/view/
   HH/fho73.html

# Index